THE HISTORY OF THE DEVIL

THE HISTORY
OF THE DEVIL

AND THE IDEA OF EVIL FROM THE EARLIEST TIMES TO THE PRESENT DAY

Paul Carus

Arnold Issac

Revitalized Occult and Strange

Contents

This edition of "THE HISTORY OF THE DEVIL AND THE IDEA OF EVIL FROM
THE EARLIEST TIMES TO THE PRESENT DAY," originally authored by Paul Carus
and published in 1900, has been revised by Arnold Issac for Revitalized Occult and
Strange, an imprint of Bald and Bonkers Network Academy LLC in 2024.

ISBN: 979-8-8691-6859-7
EISBN: 979-8-8691-6860-3

Printed 2024

1

GOOD AND EVIL AS RELIGIOUS IDEAS

Our world exhibits a dichotomy of contrasts - light and shadow, heat and cold, virtue and vice, divinity and malevolence.

This dualistic perspective on existence has marked a significant phase in the evolution of human thought. Early stages, such as Animism, prevalent across diverse cultures, introduced the notions of benevolent and malevolent spirits. Yet, a unifying tendency emerged as humanity sought coherence through Monism, favoring a singular principle. The belief in benevolent spirits leaned towards Monotheism, while the recognition of malevolent forces naturally led to the concept of a supreme evil deity embodying destructiveness and immorality.

Monotheism and Monodiabolism, products of humanity's

monistic inclinations, together construct a Dualism still embraced by many. However, this worldview isn't the culmination of philosophical inquiry. With growing awareness of the inherent Dualism within, a renewed inclination towards a higher, purely monistic perspective emerges.

Will Monism relinquish the notion of the Devil, leaving God as the singular force? Or will it abolish both, leaving only a world governed by material forces? Speculations arise about a future where religious beliefs give way to irreligion, as prophesied by M. Guyau.

Predictions of an irreligious future, where Atheism supplants various conceptions of God, are met with skepticism. The current anthropomorphic view of God, Anthropotheism, may evolve into a higher understanding where God transcends personal attributes, becoming superpersonal.

The attainment of knowledge about this superpersonal God is proposed through the scientific lens. By aligning religious inquiry with the path of science, sectarianism may evolve into a cosmical religion as broad and inclusive as science itself.

Symbols, rather than being deceptive, convey truths. As scientific understanding progresses, recognizing religious symbols in their symbolic essence won't dismantle religion but refine and liberate it from mythological trappings.

God is defined as "the authoritative presence in the All, enforcing a definite moral conduct." This presence is both immanent and transcendent, constituting universal law while also being the prerequisite for any cosmic order.

Contrary to the assertion of God's impersonality, God is superpersonal, possessing discernible qualities. While philosophers have extensively explored the concept of God, the Devil, his counterpart, remains relatively overlooked. Yet, the Devil, a multifaceted personality, may represent a reality akin to the concept of God.

Delving into demonology reveals the Devil as a complex figure, not confined to one dimension but embodying various traits, from grotesque to tragic. Much like the concept of God symbolizes a factual presence, the Devil's concept may also hold deeper realities.

The historical trajectory of demonology spans vast landscapes, necessitating volumes for comprehensive coverage. Therefore, we shall outline key features in the evolution of beliefs regarding the Devil and the nature of evil.

Across history, global cultures have grappled with the dichotomy of good and evil. The Devil, often depicted as malevolent, encapsulates the darker aspects of existence. From ancient mythologies to organized religions, the Devil features prominently in narratives explaining the origins of evil and humanity's challenges.

The notion of the Devil has evolved over time, adapting to cultural shifts and theological developments. In some traditions, the Devil is a fallen angel rebelling against divine authority; in others, it represents an inherent force within the human experience. The Devil's influence extends beyond religious doctrines, permeating literature, art, and folklore, shaping collective imagination.

As we explore demonology's historical trajectory, it becomes clear that the concept of evil is intertwined with humanity's attempts to comprehend suffering, moral ambiguity, and the darker facets of the human psyche. The Devil serves as a symbolic expression of these complex aspects of existence.

In the contemporary era, dominated by scientific and rational perspectives, the Devil may be dismissed as superstition's relic. Yet, the Devil's enduring presence in cultural narratives suggests an ongoing fascination with evil's concept and the need for symbolic representations to grapple with human nature's complexities.

In conclusion, the Devil's history and the concept of evil constitute a multifaceted journey through human thought and belief. As we navigate this intricate tapestry, it is crucial to recognize the symbolic nature of these concepts and their profound impact on shaping our understanding of morality, suffering, and the eternal struggle between light and darkness.

Footnotes:

For further exploration of these concepts, refer to the author's works, including "Idea of God," "Soul of Man" (pp. 338 et seq.), "Fundamental Problems" (p. 152 et passim), articles in "The Monist" (Vol. III., pp. 357 et seq.), and "Homilies of Science" (pp. 79-120).

2

DEVIL WORSHIP

Analyzing insights from Waitz, Lubbock, and Tylor regarding the primitive stages of religion reveals a common pattern wherein Devil-worship precedes the reverence for a benevolent Deity. Numerous instances demonstrate a transition from Devil-worship to the worship of God, with fear consistently serving as the initial impetus for religious practices. The ominous figure of the Devil, embodying a potent evil deity, prominently emerges in the early phases of various faiths. This phenomenon, known as Demonolatry or Devil-worship, signifies the initial phase in the evolution of religious beliefs, primarily motivated by apprehension of malevolence rather than an appreciation for benevolence.

Herbert Spencer's contention that savages worship the unknown encounters scrutiny. The German adage "Was die Augen nicht sehen, das betrübt das Herz nicht" (What the eyes don't see, the heart doesn't grieve for) underscores that genuinely unknowable matters are of little concern to us. Savages do not worship the unknown, such as thunder, but rather fear it due to recognized and uncontrollable hazards. The transition from Devil-worship to God-worship consistently manifests across diverse cultures.

Historical accounts of indigenous American tribes, like those in Florida and Brazil, illustrate a pronounced inclination towards Devil-worship. Even among more advanced civilizations like the Aztecs, fully relinquishing this stage of religious belief proves challenging. Human sacrifice, often associated with Devil-worship, is documented across various cultures and is even referenced in biblical texts.

As civilizations progress, modifications in sacrificial practices occur, yet vestiges of early human sacrifices endure. Myths, such as the tales of Perseus and Andromeda, reflect the transition from human to animal sacrifices. Cannibalism, frequently rooted in religious superstitions, reaches a pinnacle of abomination when associated with the belief that consuming an adversary's flesh confers virtues upon the consumer.

Traces of these ancient beliefs persist in certain interpretations of church doctrines. The dread of evil and the appeasement of wrath through bloodshed are deeply ingrained in early religious customs, gradually yielding to an acknowledgment of the positive influence of goodness. As societies evolve, the struggle against evil supplants Devil-worship, fostering confidence in the eventual triumph of justice, righteousness, and truth.

At its inception, religion is propelled by fear – fear of the unknown, fear of evil, and various endeavors to elude it. This fear-driven worship, inherent in the religions of early civilizations, evolves as human comprehension progresses. While the apprehension of evil may no longer hold as prominent a position in the religions of more advanced societies, historical inquiries reveal that malevolent powers were initially revered with awe and dread.

Devil-worship, as an early form of religion, persists until the acknowledgment of a benevolent force emerges. Experience demonstrates that despite its gradual advancement, goodness ultimately prevails. The shift transpires when the supremacy of good is recognized, and malevolent forces cease to be objects of veneration, instead becoming adversaries to be resisted, with confidence prevailing in the eventual triumph of justice, righteousness, and truth.

As societies advance, religious evolution mirrors the progress of science and philosophy, discarding primitive superstitions. Remnants of early beliefs may endure in various guises, particularly in certain interpretations of church doctrines, yet a fearless and steadfast religious reformation holds the potential to dispel these remnants.

It is imperative to acknowledge that at the early stages of religious development, certain superstitions are inevitable, akin to errors in the advancement of science and philosophy. Religion commences with fear, but as humanity advances, it metamorphoses into a pursuit of justice, a commitment to righteousness, and an unwavering dedication to truth. The historical trajectory from Devil-worship to the recognition of the triumph of goodness reflects the ongoing evolution of human spirituality and the quest for a more enlightened understanding of the divine.

The evolving comprehension of the divine is intricately linked to the progress of human thought and civilization. Early religious practices, rooted in fear and superstition, undergo transformations as societies mature. The trajectory from Devil-worship to the acknowledgment of the supremacy of goodness marks a fundamental shift in human spirituality.

As societies progress, the recognition of an absolute unknown, once central to primitive religious beliefs, gives way to a more nuanced understanding of the world. Fear, initially the driving force behind religious rituals, evolves into a deeper comprehension of the forces at play in the universe. The supernatural beings that once elicited awe and dread become symbols of moral and ethical principles, guiding humanity towards justice and righteousness.

The persistence of certain ancient beliefs in modern interpretations of religious dogmas highlights the complexity of this evolution. Fear-based rituals, including sacrifices and cannibalism, linger in symbolic forms. However, the emergence of enlightened perspectives and a fearless approach to religious reformation offers the potential for continued growth.

In the face of these changes, it becomes evident that religion is not a static entity but a dynamic force shaped by human experience and understanding. The journey from fear-driven Devil-worship to the embrace of the power of good reflects the ongoing quest for a more profound and enlightened spirituality.

As we navigate the complexities of religious evolution, it is essential to approach these narratives with a discerning and open mind. Acknowledging the historical context and the underlying human motivations behind religious practices allows for a more comprehensive understanding of the intricate tapestry of beliefs that have shaped our collective spiritual journey. The pursuit of justice, right action, and truth remains at the heart of this evolving relationship between humanity and the divine.

In this ongoing narrative of spiritual evolution, the journey from primitive fears to enlightened understanding extends beyond religious realms into the broader context of human progress. The intertwined threads of science, philosophy, and religion weave a complex tapestry that reflects our collective effort to make sense of the world.

The transition from fear-based rituals to a deeper comprehension of natural forces aligns with the parallel development of scientific inquiry. As scientific knowledge expands, the unknown becomes less a source of fear and more an invitation for exploration. The recognition that the supernatural beings of early religions were symbolic representations of moral principles reflects an evolving sophistication in ethical reasoning.

While remnants of ancient beliefs persist in contemporary interpretations, a fearless approach to religious reformation offers the potential for continued growth. The acknowledgment of past superstitions and the willingness to question and refine religious doctrines are essential components of this ongoing process.

As we reflect on the historical journey from Devil-worship to the triumph of goodness, it is crucial to recognize the adaptive nature of human spirituality. Religion, philosophy, and science are dynamic forces, shaped by the collective wisdom and experiences of diverse cultures. The quest for justice, ethical conduct, and truth emerges as a common thread uniting these diverse aspects of human inquiry.

In the modern era, the dialogue between religion and science need not be one of conflict but of mutual enrichment. A holistic understanding of the universe, encompassing both the spiritual and the empirical, can foster a more comprehensive worldview. The journey towards an enlightened spirituality involves embracing the positive aspects of our religious heritage while discarding the outdated and fear-driven elements.

As humanity continues its exploration of the unknown, the narrative of spiritual evolution unfolds. It is a story of resilience, adaptability, and the pursuit of higher truths that transcend the primitive fears of the past. In this ongoing journey, the potential for a more harmonious coexistence between science, philosophy, and religion becomes a beacon guiding us towards a future enriched by the collective wisdom of the ages.

The harmonious coexistence of science, philosophy, and religion in the ongoing human journey reflects a maturation of our collective consciousness. This journey is marked by the gradual integration of diverse perspectives and a growing recognition that each facet contributes uniquely to our understanding of existence.

Science, with its empirical methods, continues to unravel the mysteries of the natural world, offering insights into the workings of the universe. Simultaneously, philosophy provides a space for contemplation and introspection, delving into the profound questions of purpose and meaning. Religion, in its refined form, serves as a source of ethical guidance, moral principles, and a framework for the human experience.

As we navigate this intricate interplay, the narrative of spiritual evolution becomes not just a historical account but a roadmap for the future. The journey involves acknowledging the shadows of the past, confronting superstitions, and embracing a more nuanced understanding of the divine. This ongoing process allows for the preservation of valuable ethical teachings while discarding the fear-based elements that hinder progress.

The dialogue between science and religion, often portrayed as adversarial, can be transformative when viewed as a symbiotic relationship. Science, with its capacity for observation and discovery, enriches religious understanding by demystifying natural phenomena. Simultaneously, religion contributes to the human experience by providing moral frameworks, fostering a sense of community, and addressing existential questions that science alone may not fully answer.

In the quest for an enlightened spirituality, a fearless and open-minded approach becomes paramount. This entails embracing the diversity of human beliefs, recognizing the limitations of our current understanding, and fostering a spirit of curiosity that transcends rigid dogmas.

As we stand at the intersection of ancient wisdom and modern knowledge, the narrative of spiritual evolution calls for a collective effort to build bridges between different ways of understanding the world. In doing so, we can cultivate a more holistic worldview that honors both the empirical and the contemplative, fostering a richer tapestry of human experience and wisdom.

Footnotes

1. Tylor, "Primitive Culture," II., p. 325.

2. "A map of Virginia. With a description of the covntrey, etc., written by Captaine Smith, etc. Oxford. Printed by Joseph Barnes. 1612."

3. In the small dictionary of the language of the Virginia savages, printed in the same pamphlet, Captain Smith translates "Oke" simply by "gods."

4. Arber, Edward (ed.). "The Works of Capt. John Smith of Willoughby, etc.," Birmingham, 1884, pp. 74 ff.

5. "The Religious Ceremonies and Customs of the Several Nations of the Known World," III., p. 129.

6. See original author's work, "De rebus oceanicis et novo orbe."

3

ANCIENT EGYPT

Set is often juxtaposed with Osiris. Set, the deity associated with the desert, drought, and arid climates, embodies destruction, whereas Osiris symbolizes moisture, the Nile, and life-sustaining energies. According to Plutarch:

"Osiris, depicted by the moon, emanates nurturing light conducive to animal and plant growth. Conversely, Typhon, represented by the sun, exerts relentless scorching heat, rendering portions of the earth inhospitable and occasionally overpowering even Osiris, symbolized by the moon."

Set, as a force antithetical to life, is linked with destruction, which extends to the waning moon, the receding Nile waters, and the setting sun. Termed as the left or black eye of the declining sun, Set governs from the summer solstice to the winter solstice. This contrasts with Hor's right or bright eye, symbolizing the ascending sun, growth, and the diffusion of light from the winter to the summer solstice.

In ancient Egypt, Set was not universally perceived as a Satanic figure. He commanded an official following in a relatively minor province west of the Nile, a region serving as a natural hub for the route to the northern oasis. The inhabitants, primarily guides for desert caravans, had pragmatic motives to maintain amicable relations with Set, the ruler of the desert.

Moreover, historical records unveil a notable temple dedicated to Set as the god of war in Tanis, situated near the swamps amidst the eastern branches of the Delta. This locale held strategic importance as a frontier town and potentially served as the seat of foreign authority during the Hyksos and Hyttite invasions. Even among the Hyksos, Set was revered as a formidable deity associated with brute force, warfare, and devastation.

In an ancient mural at Karnak from the eighteenth dynasty, Set is depicted imparting archery skills to King Thothmes III.

Sety I, the second ruler of the nineteenth dynasty, often linked with the shepherd kings, derived his name from the god Set, indicating the high regard in which he was held among the shepherd kings. Historical evidence suggests that these rulers regarded Set, or Sutech, as the sole deity worthy of divine homage, considering him the supreme god.

Associating the era of the shepherd kings with the settlement of Jacob's sons in Egypt and perceiving the monotheism of the Hyksos as the precursor to Moses's religion evokes intriguing considerations. The reverence elicited by a formidable power among the Egyptians metamorphoses into the demonization of Set and among the Israelites into the worship of Yahveh.

Despite the fear he instilled, Set was not initially perceived solely as an evil demon; rather, he was one of the revered great deities, both feared and appeased. According to Heinrich Brugsch (Religion und Mythologie der alten Aegypter, p. 706):

"The Book of the Dead of the ancient Egyptians and the numerous inscriptions of the recently opened pyramids primarily functioned as talismans against the imagined Seth and his accomplices. Unfortunately, much of the ancient literature we possess adheres to this trend."

In Egyptian belief, upon death, an individual traverses the western horizon and descends into Amenti, the Nether World, through Atmu's abode. The preservation of their "double" or "other self" in the tomb, typically in the mummy or a statue of their likeness, is pivotal for the salvation of their essence.

The double, treated as if alive, purportedly requires sustenance provided through incantations. Magical formulas alleviate hunger and thirst within the tomb, thwarting the malevolent intentions of Set and his cohorts. An inscription from Edfu reads:

"Hail Ra, thou art radiant in thy radiance,
"While there is darkness in the eyes of Apophis!
"Hail Ra, good is thy goodness,
"While Apophis is bad in its badness!"

The perpetual dread of hunger, thirst, and potential harm to the double in the tomb haunted every devout Egyptian. This apprehension prompted the practice of embalming the deceased and the construction of pyramids. Despite superstitions and elaborate burial rites, inscriptions indicate that many discerning individuals believed that leading a righteous life offered the best, if not the sole, safeguard against typhonic influences after death. Chapter CXXV of the Book of the Dead exemplifies this conviction, as per Lepsius's edition of the Turin papyrus.

The Hall of Truth, depicted in the Turin papyrus, portrays Osiris donning the atef-crown, crook, and whip. Above him loom the genii Shai and Ranen, embodying Misery and Happiness. Hovering over an altar laden with offerings are four funerary genii—Amset, Hapi, Tuamutef, and Kebhsnauf. A frieze showcases twelve sets of uraeus snakes, flames, and feathers of truth. Positioned on either side, baboons sacred to Thoth hold scales poised at the midpoint, where Atmu extends hands over the right and left eye, symbolizing sunset and sunrise, death and rebirth.

The goddess of truth, Mâ, adorned with an erect feather, guides the departed into the Hall of Truth. Kneeling, the departed invokes the forty-two assessors by name and denies transgressing any of the forty-two sins in the Egyptian moral code. Confessions extracted include:

"I did not commit evil—I did not perpetrate violence—I did not cause distress to any heart—I did not steal—I did not orchestrate treacherous killings—I did not diminish offerings—I did not inflict harm—I did not utter falsehoods—I did not cause others to weep—I did not engage in impurity—I did not commit adultery—I did not encroach—I did not deceive—I did not harm cultivated land—I did not slander—I did not harbor unfounded anger—I did not disregard the truth—I did not practice sorcery—I did not blaspheme—I did not mal-treat a slave—I did not scorn God in my heart."

Subsequently, the departed places their heart on the bal-ance of truth, assessed by the hawk-headed Hor and the jackal-headed Anubis. Thoth, the ibis-headed scribe of the gods, relays Hor's findings to Osiris. If the heart's weight aligns with truth, Thoth orders its reinstatement within the departed's chest, symbolizing a return to life. Evading perils in the descent to Amenti and possessing an unblemished heart, the departed can embark on the "boat of the sun," journeying to the Elysian fields of the blessed.

From a contemporary viewpoint, if an individual's mis-deeds outweigh their virtuous deeds, they face consumption by Amemit, also known as "the beast of Amenti," or are re-incarnated in the upper world in the form of a pig.

While the double remains in the tomb, the soul, depicted as a bird with a human head, ascends to the heavens, merging with the great gods. The liberated soul proclaims (Erman, ib., p. 343 et seq.):

"I am the god Atum, I who was alone,

"I am the god Ra at his first appearing,

"I am the great god who created himself, and created his name Lord of the gods, who has not his equal.'

"I was yesterday, and I know the tomorrow. The battle-field of the gods was made when I spoke.

"I come into my home, I come into my native city.

"I commune daily with my father Atum.

"My impurities are driven out, and the sin that was in me is conquered.

"Ye gods above, reach out your hands, I am like you, I have become one of you.

"I commune daily with my father Atum.

Having merged with the gods, the departed soul undergoes a fate akin to Osiris. Like Osiris, it is slain by Set and reborn in Hor, who avenges his father's death. Simultaneously, the soul is believed to frequently visit the double of the departed in the tomb, as depicted in the tomb of the scribe Ani.

The Abode of Bliss (Sechnit aanru in Egyptian, also written aahlu), portrayed in the Turin papyrus of the Book of the Dead, depicts the departed alongside their family, accompanied by Thoth, the scribe of the gods, presenting offerings to three gods adorned with the feather of truth. Crossing the waters, the departed offers a censer to their soul, appearing as a man-headed bird. The illustration includes scenes of plowing, sowing, reaping, and thanksgiving, alongside boats for Ra Harmakhis and Unefru, and three islands representing Ra, the regenerative abode of the gods, and the dwelling of Shu, Tefnut, and Seb.

An insightful representation of Egyptian belief is found in the well-preserved tomb of Rekhmara, the prefect of Thebes under Thothmes III of the eighteenth dynasty. Translated by Ph. Virey, the tomb's inscriptions depict Rekhmara's transition from life to death and subsequent resurrection, symbolizing the cyclic nature of existence.

In Rekhmara's tomb, Set receives offerings alongside other eminent gods, and the departed is hailed as the inheritor of Set, purged by both Hor and Set. Embodied in Osiris, the departed is approached and slain by Set, who is then defeated in the form of sacrificial beasts. Following the restoration of the departed's faculties and mental acuity, Set continues to play a significant role, appearing as one of the four cardinal points alongside Hor, Thoth, and Seb.

Initially symbolizing the sunset and the death of the sun, Set gradually metamorphosed into a demonic entity with the ascendance of Osiris worship. The reign of Men-Kau-Ra, the constructor of the third pyramid of Gizeh, signaled a shift in Egyptian religious beliefs, introducing the concept of the justified soul merging with Osiris, as reflected in the prayer on his coffin lid.

Over time, Set's status as a deity dwindled, and during the twenty-second dynasty, efforts were made to expunge his name from inscriptions, indicative of growing confidence in the supremacy of gods associated with benevolence and virtue.

Plutarch, reflecting on his era, notes the waning power of Typhon (Set), occasionally humiliated during festivals. Once an imposing deity, Set evolved into a symbol of malevolence and demonization, forfeiting divine reverence as Osiris worship gained ascendancy.

In essence, Set, originally a potent deity, underwent a transformation into a malevolent figure as Osiris worship prevailed. Central themes in Egyptian beliefs—life and death cycles, the journey of the soul, and the struggle between good and evil—involve Set in the cosmic order despite his diminishing divine stature.

Footnotes

1. Lepsius, Denkmäler, Vol. V., p. 36. The illustration

is elucidated by Adolf Erman in his work "Life in Ancient Egypt," English translation, p. 282.

2. Also known as Maâ't, or "the two truths," representing the upper and lower worlds.

3. Ph. Virey's "Le Tombeau de Rakhmara." Paris: Le Roux. 1889.

4

ACCAD AND THE
EARLY SEMITES

Around the year 3000 B.C., well before the emergence
of Semitic nations like Babylonians, Assyrians, Israelites, and
later the Arabians, there thrived a powerful and significant
civilization in Mesopotamia known as Accad. Interestingly,
the Accadians were not a white race but rather a dark one,
often referred to as "blackheads" or "blackfaces." However,
they were likely more reddish-dark or brown, as indicated by
the term "Adamatu" or red-skins found in bilingual tablets.

The Accadian influence on Semitic cultures, even after
their dominion ended around 1500 B.C., is profound. Many
religious institutions, legends, and customs among the Sem-
ites have roots in Accadian origins. For instance, the Accadians already had a seven-day week and observed the Sabbath

as a holy day of rest, with the term Sabbath meaning "a day on which work is unlawful."

Accadian traditions also left a mark on creation legends, the tree of life, and the deluge, shared between Genesis and Assyrian records. The tree of life, often depicted with fir-cones, hints at an ancient tradition from the fir-covered mountains of Media, the Accadians' former home.

Hebrew names and the rivers of paradise in Genesis also bear reminiscences of Accadian influence, suggesting a lasting impact on ancient civilizations. Notably, the rivers of Eden have Babylonian names, and the cultivated portion of the desert lands west of the Euphrates was called Edinna, resembling Eden.

The insights of Berosus, a Babylonian priest from the time of Alexander the Great, further corroborate Accadian traditions, providing a valuable historical and religious perspective on Babylon. The excavations of Assyrian stone-libraries have solidified the reliability and ancient origins of these traditions, emphasizing the enduring legacy of the Accadians.

The Babylonians had several legends that made their way into the Old Testament. Notable among them are the stories of the deluge, the tower of Babel, the destruction of corrupt cities by a rain of fire (reminiscent of Sodom and Gomorrah), the early adventures of King Sargon I (similar to Moses), and the creation of the world. The name Babel, Assyrian bab-ilani or bab-ilu, meaning "Gate of God," is a Semitic translation of the Accadian Ka-dingirra-ki with the same meaning, literally "Gate + of God + the place." The proposed etymology of Babel from balbel, meaning "to confound," in both the

Assyrian account and Genesis is an etymological error found in ancient texts.

The legend of the destruction of cities includes Accadian names, indicating an Accadian source. The deluge legend aligns closely with the Genesis story and is the eleventh part of an epic celebrating Izdubar, an Assyrian Hercules, traveling through the twelve signs of the Zodiac, with the eleventh corresponding to the "rainy" month in Accadian tradition.

Even in modern cathedrals, depictions of the four Evangelists often feature representative beings of the animal creation. Matthew is paired with an angel or winged man, Mark with a lion, Luke with a steer, and St. John with an eagle. These creatures symbolize the cherubim from the Old Testament, viewed by early Christians as guardians and heavenly prototypes of Gospel writers. However, these symbols predate Jewish tradition and are found on the walls of ancient royal palaces in Nineveh, suggesting an even more ancient origin than the Old Testament itself.

Regarding Sargon I, the king of Agade, who, according to a tablet of King Nabonidus, lived around 3754 B.C. and erected a temple to Samas, E. A. Wallis Budge, in Babylonian Life and History (p. 40), shares an intriguing legend about him:

"There's an interesting legend about this king, suggesting he was born in a city on the banks of the Euphrates. His mother, conceiving him in secret, gave birth to him in a humble place, placed him in a pitch-sealed ark, and cast him upon the river. The river carried him along until a man named Akki rescued him, raising him in his own trade. From this position, the goddess Ishtar eventually made him a king."

The origin of these legends can be traced to Assyrio-

Babylonian roots. Well-respected authorities confirm that Chaldea was the birthplace of these stories, and the Jews likely inherited them from the Babylonians. Ancient seals from Assyria and Babylon, discovered in excavations, demonstrate that these legends were well-known and part of the region's literature before the second millennium B.C.

It's likely that various versions of the old Chaldean legends existed. We have two accounts of the creation story, one narrated on seven tablets, which is particularly significant. It serves as a primary source for the first chapter of the Old Testament and introduces one of the oldest documents mentioning the existence of the Evil One, referred to as Tiamtu in Assyrian—symbolized as the serpent beating the sea, the serpent of the night, the serpent of darkness, the wicked serpent, and the mighty and strong serpent.

The influence of Assyrian sources on the biblical account of Creation is unmistakable, evident not only in significant similarities but also in the use of identical words in Genesis and Assyrian inscriptions. Shared elements include the creation of woman from the rib of man and the sending out of birds from the ark to check if the waters had subsided. Coincidences even extend to specific words like Mehûmâh (confusion, chaos) in Hebrew matching Assyrian Mummu, and tehôm (the deep) and tohû (desolate) aligning with Assyrian Tiamtu (= Tiamat).

While there's no discovered report of the fall of man and the serpent tempting Adam and Eve to eat from the tree of life, the presence of similar legends is probable. Artifacts depict two figures seated under a tree with a serpent nearby, suggesting the existence of a comparable tale.

The concept of the tree of life was highly popular among the Assyrians and Babylonians, evident in various artistic depictions. It likely originated from a time when the fruits of trees played a vital role in sustaining human life.

Tiamat, the original watery chaos giving rise to heaven and earth, held diverse roles in Babylonian thought. Philosophers viewed Tiamat as the mother of the world and the source of all things. In mythology, however, it represented disorder and served as the mother of the deep's monsters.

A significant shift in this chaotic narrative occurred when Tiamat was eventually conquered in a fierce battle, as recounted in the fourth tablet of the creation story, by the Sun-god, Belus or Bel-Merodach. Yet, the struggle persisted, and Bel had to combat seven wicked storm-demons darkening the moon. He engaged in battles against dragons and evil spirits, symbolizing the return of divine intelligence through a myth where Bel commanded a god to cut off his head. This head, representing Bel's, was mixed with the earth to create animals capable of enduring the light.

In summary, the Babylonian creation story unfolds with Tiamat playing a crucial role. Professor Sayce explains that the initial tablet presents cosmological doctrines, revealing a watery chaos, Mummu Tiamat, from which gods and the created world emerged. The struggle against Tiamat and the subsequent creation of the heavens, celestial bodies, and the earth form the subsequent tablets. The epic parallels the biblical account in its seven-act structure and the precedence of a watery chaos, although differences exist.

Notably, the struggle between Merodach and the powers of evil in the Babylonian story finds a parallel in biblical verses about a war in heaven. The worship of multiple deities, including the favorite god Bel (identified with Merodach), reflects Babylonian beliefs. The Babylonian trinity of Anu, Ea, and Bel, often depicted above the tree of life, signifies divine balance. Bel-Merodach's struggles and triumphs against Tiamat contribute to the complexity of Babylonian cosmology and mythology, showcasing the enduring influence of these ancient narratives.

Bel-Merodach, described as the Christ figure in Babylonian beliefs, is portrayed as the son of Ea, representing all knowledge and wisdom. According to Professor Budge, Merodach, also known as Marduk, is considered omnipresent and omnipotent, serving as a mediator for humanity and a healer. He reveals the knowledge of Ea, and people invoke him as the powerful god who safeguards against evil.

The artistic depiction of the conflict between Bel-Merodach and Tiamat, a popular theme among Assyrian artists, often represents the Evil One as a monstrous being with claws, horns, tail, wings, and scales. This visual representation adds a vivid dimension to the mythology.

Regarding the Babylonian concept of the Evil One and their version of hell, Mr. Budge draws parallels to biblical references. Babylonian Hades, similar to Sheol in the Bible, is portrayed with a river, a ferryman, and seven gates. The descent of Istar to the Babylonian Hades in search of her husband, Tammuz, is detailed in a tablet. The land of no return, the dwelling of the deity Irkalla, is described as a place of corruption and darkness, with spirits crossing the river and encountering gates guarded by a porter. The tablet vividly illustrates the challenges faced by Istar on her journey, emphasizing the eerie atmosphere and the presence of the dead.

The Babylonian conception of hell, or Arali as another name suggests, mirrors some aspects of biblical Sheol. Though it is unclear where the Babylonians believed Hades to be, some conjecture places it in the west. The tablet provides valuable insights into their perception of the afterlife, revealing a realm filled with darkness, dust, and spectral entities.

This Babylonian underworld was guarded by a formidable porter, and Istar, the daughter of the Moon-god, describes her determination to gain entry. The verses vividly convey the urgency and power she claims, threatening to force open the gates, shatter bolts, strike thresholds, and cross doors. The language paints a haunting picture of a realm where the dead outnumber the living, where inhabitants consume dust and mud as their sustenance, and where perpetual darkness prevails.

The Babylonian Hades, with its intricate details and vivid descriptions, showcases a complex mythology and a belief system that incorporates elements of the divine, the supernatural, and the afterlife. The parallels drawn between the Babylonian concepts and biblical references, such as Sheol, add layers of intrigue to our understanding of ancient beliefs.

The tablet also hints at the uncertainty regarding the exact location of this underworld, with some speculating it to be in the west. Despite the geographical ambiguity, the rich imagery and symbolism embedded in the Babylonian portrayal of the afterlife provide a glimpse into the intricate tapestry of their religious and mythological perspectives. These beliefs, entwined with the struggles of deities like Bel-Merodach

against forces of chaos and darkness, contribute to the richness of Babylonian cosmology and underscore the timeless
human fascination with the mysteries of existence beyond
the mortal realm.

According to Mr. Budge, when it comes to the concept
of the Evil One and hell in Babylonian beliefs (pages 139
and 140):

"Their version of Hades wasn't all that different from
Sheol or the 'pit' mentioned in the Bible, and the Devil wasn't
distinctly separate from the Satan we're familiar with."

Details about the Babylonian vision of hell come from
a tablet recounting Istar's descent in search of her beloved
young husband, Tammuz. Although claims have been made
that the same term for Hades, Sheol in Hebrew Scriptures,
is found in Babylonian texts, there's currently no definitive
evidence to support this. In Babylonian Hades, also known
as the land of no return, the lady, Nin-kigal, presided. The
place featured a river that spirits had to traverse, reminiscent
of the Greek Charon, and it was guarded by a porter of the
waters at its seven gates.

The tablet narrates:

1. To the land of no return, to the far-off, to regions of
corruption,

2. Istar, the daughter of the Moon-god, her attention
firmly

3. fixed, the daughter of the Moon-god, her attention
fixed

4. the house of corruption, the dwelling of the deity
Irkalla (to go)

5. to the house whose entrance is without exit

6. to the road whose way is without return

7. to the house whose entrance is bereft of light

8. a place where much dust is their food, their meat mud,

9. where light is never seen, where they dwell in darkness

10. ghosts (?) like birds whirl round and round the vaults

11. over the doors and wainscoting there is thick dust.

The outer gate of this 'land of no return' was securely guarded, and when the porter initially denied Istar entry, she declared:

"Open thy gate and let me enter in;
If thou openest not the gate, and I come not in,
I force the gate, the bolt I shatter,
I strike the threshold, and I cross the doors,
I raise the dead, devourers of the living,
(for) the dead exceed the living."

Another name for Hades is mentioned, with its signs forming the meaning 'the house of the land of the dead,' and its pronunciation given as Arali. The exact location of their imagined Hades remains uncertain, with some speculating it might be in the west.

In addition to Tiamat, Assyrian and Babylonian mythology introduced a plethora of demons, whose names are documented in inscriptions and whose likenesses are preserved on various artifacts like statues, bas-reliefs, and cylinders. The magic incantations used to repel their influence were consistently recited seven times in the Sumero-Accadian language, revered for its antiquity. Although it had become unintelligible to the common people, it persisted for liturgical purposes. The Assyrians believed that exposing demons to their own forms and urging them to self-destruct in internal conflicts would scare them away.

Lenormant succinctly outlines Assyrian demonology in "Histoire ancienne de l'Orient," Vol. V, page 494.

"In both the Good and Evil forces, a hierarchical system of spirits exists based on their rank. The texts mention ekim and telal as warriors, maskin as trappers, alal as destroyers, and labartu, labassu, and ahharu as various types of ghosts, phantoms, and vampires. The mas, lamma, and utuq are frequently cited, distinguishing between good and evil variations of these entities. Additionally, there are alapi, winged bulls, nirgalli, winged lions, and numerous types of heavenly archangels. The gods Anna and Ea, known as the spirit of heaven (zi an na) and the spirit of the earth (zi ki a), are commonly invoked in incantations for protection against evil spirits. Chaldean monuments reveal an extremely intricate demonology, the precise hierarchy of which is not yet fully understood."

Regarding the demon associated with the disease-inducing southwest wind, Lenormant notes (ibid. V., p. 212):

"The Louvre houses an image of a fearsome demon standing upright with a dog's head, eagle's feet, lion's paws, and a scorpion's tail. Half of the head exposes a fleshless skull, and it has four wings spread out. An inscription in Sumero-

Accadian on the statue indicates that it represents the demon of the southwest wind and should be placed at doors or windows to ward off its harmful influence. The southwest wind in Chaldea originates from the Arabian deserts, carrying a scorching breath that causes damage similar to the khamsin in Syria and the simoon in Africa."

The Nirgalli, as described by the same scholar (ibid. V., p. 215), were depicted in the palace of Asurbanipal at Kuyunjik. These creatures, with human bodies, lion heads, and eagle feet, engaged in combat with each other using daggers and clubs. They represented demons and conveyed the sculptor's message often found in incantations: 'The evil demons should get out, they should mutually kill one another.'"

An ancient bronze tablet portrays a depiction of the world gripped by the Devil. Lenormant, discussing the Chaldean concept of hell, refers to this notable piece of antiquity, describing it as follows:

"A bronze plate in the collection of M. De Clercq contains in a synoptic world-picture a representation of hell, and it is necessary that we here give a description of it. One side of the bronze plate is entirely occupied by a four-footed monster, with four wings, standing on eagle's claws. Raising himself on his hind feet, he looks as though he intended to jump over the plate against which he leans. His head reaches over the border as over the top of a wall. The face of the wild and roaring monster towers, on the other side of the plate, above a picture which is divided into four horizontal strips representing the heavens, the earth, and hell. In the top strip, one sees the symbolic representations of the celestial bodies. Underneath appears a series of seven persons clad in long robes and having beads of a lion, a dog, a bear, a ram, a horse, an eagle, and a serpent. These are the celestial genii called ighigs. The third strip exhibits a funeral scene, which undoubtedly happens on earth. Two personages dressed in the skin of a fish, after the fashion of the god Anu, are standing at the head and foot of a mummy. Further on there are two genii— one with a lion's head, the other with a jackal's head—who threaten one another with their daggers, and a man seems to flee from this scene of horror. The picture of the fourth strip is bathed in the floods of the ocean, which according to the traditional mythology of the Chaldeans reaches underneath the foundations of the earth. An ugly monster, half bestial, half human, with eagle's wings and claws, and a tail terminating in a snake's head, stands on the shore of the ocean, on which a boat is floating. This is the boat of the deity Elippu, frequently mentioned in the religious texts and probably the prototype of the boat of Charon in Greek mythology. In the boat is a horse which carries upon its back a gigantic lion-headed deity, holding in her hands two serpents; and two little lions jump to her breast to suck her milk. In the corner there are fragments of all kinds, human limbs, vases, and the remainders of a feast.

"Thus, this little bronze tablet contains the picture of the world such as the imagination of the Chaldeans represented it: the gods and the sidereal powers, angels and demons, ighigs and anunnaks, the earth and men, with supernatural beings who exercise a direct influence upon them; the dead protected by certain demons and attacked by others according to the philosophical conception of good and evil, and the antagonism of the two principles which constitute the basis of the Assyrio-Chaldean religion. Anu protects the dead in the same way as does the Egyptian Osiris. There is the subterranean river reminding one of the Styx and Acheron of the Greeks as well as of the subterranean Nile of Amenti." (P. 291.)

Undoubtedly, the ancient biblical legends, rather than diminishing in significance with their proven antiquity, have gained added value, becoming even more intriguing to us. While the biblical creation account was previously perceived as the initial stage in the religious evolution of humanity, we now recognize it as merely a marker on the journey. It is neither the beginning nor the end; it is essentially a summary of a protracted history of inquisitive exploration and speculation. This history would have remained concealed if not for the Assyrian tablets attesting to the aspirations preceding the compilation of the Old Testament. Yet, an intriguing aspect emerges: the Chaldean belief in the immortality of the soul did not find resonance in Jewish literature. Did the Jews omit it from the Hebrew worldview because they doubted it, or did they overlook it due to their pragmatic outlook, resisting being swayed by even the loftiest illusions?

Despite Assyria and Babylon boasting a more vibrant, powerful, and cosmopolitan civilization than Israel, a crucial distinction exists in the religious legends and theories of these two nations. While Assyrian tablets are polytheistic and mythological, the Hebrew text is monotheistic. The mythological embellishments of the original story have been tempered and simplified. Without disregarding the poetic beauty of the original, which, in its way, is as venerable as the later Hebrew version, the latter represents a definite improvement. Its greater simplicity and freedom from fantastical details imbue it with a distinctive sobriety and grandeur entirely absent in the Assyrian myth of creation.

While acknowledging the superiority of the Hebrew narrative, it is important to note, in fairness to Assyrian and Babylonian civilization, that monotheism was not an exclusively Jewish belief. Long before the existence of the Israelites, Egypt and Babylon featured monotheistic hymns of considerable strength and religious beauty. The "monotheistic party" of Babylon, as identified by Sir Henry Rawlinson, or its counterparts in Egypt, may well have laid the foundations of Jewish monotheism. The influence of Egyptian and Babylonian philosophers on the development of Israelitic religion is evident.

Egyptian and Babylonian monotheists seemingly tolerated popular mythology as a symbolic expression of religious truth. In later periods, Jewish religious leaders, intolerant of polytheism, succeeded in eradicating popular superstitions from their sacred literature. Some vestiges, now valuable hints, remain, providing insight into the nature of the text before the hands of later redactors altered it.

Footnotes

1. A commonly held etymology links the word "Adamatu" to "Adamu" or "Admu," meaning "man." This later reappears in the Bible as the name of the first man. Refer to George Smith's "The Chaldean Account of Genesis" for details (p. 83).

2. Sir Henry Rawlinson suggests that "Gân Eden" or the "Garden of Eden" is synonymous with "Gan-Duniyas" (also

known as "Gan-Duni"), meaning "enclosure," a name for Babylonia found in Assyrian inscriptions.

3. For further insights, see Cory's "Ancient Fragments" (pp. 51-56).

4. Refer to George Smith's "The Chaldean Account of Genesis," edited by Prof. A. H. Sayce (p. 304), and Dr. Paul Haupt's habilitation lecture "Der keilinschriftliche Sintfluth-bericht," Leipzig, 1881.

5. Although commonly referred to as Gilgamesh, the proper transcription is "Gilgamesh." He is also known as "Gistubar," with the literal meaning of the word being "mass of fire." Explore Lenormant's "Histoire Ancienne de l'Orient," V., p. 199.

6. Some Zodiac depictions bear a striking resemblance to modern charts. For instance, the centaur and scorpion can be observed on an Assyrian bas-relief in the British Museum (Lenormant's "Histoire Ancienne de l'Orient," V., p. 180).

7. Noteworthy etymological connections include "fagus" (beechtree) and "φηγός" (oak), both related to the English word "beech" and the German "Buche," meaning "eating" or "the tree with eatable fruit." The term "acorn," unrelated to oak, is connected to "acre," meaning "harvest or fruit." It is distinct from the German "Eichel" (acorn) but shares similarity with "Ecker," the name for beechtree fruit.

5

PERSIAN DUALISM

The shift from Devil-worship to God-worship signifies the dawn of civilization, and among ancient nations, the Persians appear to be the pioneers in this conscious transition. They emphasized the dichotomy between good and evil so fervently that their religion is still considered the most coherent form of dualism.

The initiator of Persian dualism was Zarathustra, also known as "Zoroaster" in Greek, a name literally translating to "golden splendor." Zoroaster, the prominent prophet of Mazdaism, the belief in Mazda, the Omniscient One, is seen as the concluding link in a chain of earlier prophets. When he emerged, the conditions were ripe for the transformative movement, indicating that others had paved the way for his teachings.

Although later writings depict Zoroaster as a demigod, suggesting a mythical figure, the "Gathas" provide documentary evidence of his real historical existence. Scholars like Prof. A. V. Williams Jackson and Dr. E. W. West date Zoroaster to the latter half of the seventh and the middle of the sixth century. The introduction of the Zoroastrian calendar reform in 505 B.C. further supports that the kings of the Achæmenian dynasty were Zoroastrians.

Zoroaster's zealous ministry is believed to have occurred in the kingdom of Bactria, where he found fertile ground for spreading his teachings. The Bactrian king Vishtaspa played a crucial role in supporting the Zoroastrian crusade that extended the new faith across eastern Iran. This religious war faced challenges, including a conflict with Turan, the same race blamed for the death of Cyrus. Despite a momentary setback, the spiritual regeneration persisted, eventually turning into the flame of Persian power that triumphed over decaying Media and illuminated the early history of Iran.

This resurgence of Zoroastrianism, marked by the zeal of Zarathustra and the support of kings like Vishtaspa, sparked a spiritual and cultural transformation in Persia. The Gathas, although limited in details about Zoroaster's life, affirm his historical presence, challenging the notion of his purely mythical status.

Zoroaster's teachings found resonance in the receptive soil of eastern Iran, particularly in Bactria. The Bactrian king's endorsement and active support facilitated the rapid spread of the new faith. References to this crusade permeate Zoroastrian literature, underscoring its significance in reshaping the religious landscape.

The clash with Turan, a historical adversary linked to Cyrus's demise, symbolized a momentary setback. Tradition speaks of Balkh's storming, where the sacred altar's fire was said to be extinguished in the blood of priests. Yet, this defeat was a precursor to victory, as the spiritual spark endured, ready to ignite the flame of Persian dominance.

The narrative, often laden with symbolic language, mirrors the broader historical context. The spiritual regeneration persisted amidst challenges, turning adversity into a force propelling the ascendancy of Persian power. The transformation extended beyond religion, shaping the destiny of the land of Iran.

Zoroaster, though possibly born in Atropatene, found his prophetic mission in Bactria, weaving a narrative of reform and a nobler faith. The echoes of his teachings resonated far beyond his homeland, shaping the course of history and solidifying the foundations of Zoroastrianism, a pivotal chapter in the evolution of ancient civilizations.

The Gathas, hymns originating from the fifth and sixth centuries BCE, carry authenticity confirmed not only by later Persian literature like the Pahlavi books but also by Greek sources. Authors such as Plutarch and Diogenes Laertes, quoting Theopompus from the late fourth century BCE, contribute to the validation of the Gathas.

Attributed to Zoroaster, these hymns portray him not as a demigod but as a human wrestling with the complexities of his prophetic mission. Zoroaster, reflected in the Gathas, experiences moments of elation fueled by grand aspirations and, at times, doubts about the ultimate success of his devoted movement. L. H. Mill, the Gathas' translator, emphasizes the authenticity of these hymns, emphasizing their connection to an ongoing religious movement.

According to Prof. Mill, the Gathas' doctrines and exhortations directly relate to a contemporary religious movement, characterized by exceptional purity and sincerity. The idea of forgery or an attempt to impose doctrines on the sacred community in Zoroaster's name, as seen in later texts, is ruled out for the Gathas.

In Zoroaster's time, two religious factions existed: worshippers of daêvas or nature-gods and those devoted to Ahura, the Lord. The Gathas present Zoroaster as a high-ranking priest who emerged as the leader of the Ahura party. Zoroaster not only demoted the old nature-gods, the daêvas, to demonic status but also identified them as representatives of a malevolent force named Angrô Mainyush or Ahriman, signifying "the evil spirit," and Druj, meaning falsehood.

Zoroaster's pivotal role in the Gathas extends beyond the theological debates of his time. As a priest of the highest order, he assumed leadership in the Ahura party, a faction that stood in stark contrast to the worshippers of daêvas or nature-gods. Within the Gathas, Zoroaster not only cast down the old nature-gods, reclassifying them as demons, but he also framed them as agents of a malevolent force he termed Angrô Mainyush or Ahriman, denoting "the evil spirit," and Druj, representing falsehood.

These hymns provide a glimpse into Zoroaster's inner struggles. They portray him not as an infallible deity but as a human grappling with the grandiosity of his prophetic mission. Zoroaster's emotional journey is evident as he fluctuates between confidence in his divine calling and moments of doubt regarding the movement's ultimate success.

The Gathas' authenticity, affirmed by Persian and Greek

sources, dismisses any notion of forgery or manipulation. The hymns serve as a sincere reflection of an ongoing religious movement characterized by purity and earnestness, distinct from later texts that might have carried different motives.

Zoroaster's legacy extends beyond his time, shaping the religious landscape and influencing subsequent philosophical and theological developments. The Gathas, rooted in the struggles and convictions of a historical figure, continue to stand as a testament to the evolving narrative of faith and human introspection.

In the vast plains of Northern Asia, the Scythians, formidable neighbors of Persia, revered their supreme deity with the symbol of a serpent. Unsurprisingly, this serpent, Afrasiâb, later became synonymous with the archfiend Ahriman, embodying the adversary god of the Persians.

Contrary to a common misconception, the Persians are not accurately labeled as fire worshippers. Zoroaster's teachings clarified that the sun, devoid of inherent divinity, shouldn't receive direct worship. Similarly, the lit flame, an homage to Ahura Mazda, symbolizes the light of the soul and the embodiment of all goodness.

Zoroaster's doctrine rejects the notion that Ahura created Ahriman; instead, the evil spirit possesses independent existence. While Ahriman lacks equal dignity and power compared to the Lord, both are considered creative and uncreated, representing opposing principles. This fundamental dualism in Persian religion finds explicit expression in the thirtieth Yasna:

"Two primeval spirits, well known, correlated yet independent; one embodies the better, the other the worse, in thought, word, and deed. Let the wise choose rightly between these two."

This dualistic perspective underlines a crucial aspect of Zoroastrianism. The contrasting principles of the better and the worse, embodied by Ahura Mazda and Ahriman, extend beyond mere philosophical abstraction. They manifest in the choices individuals make in their thoughts, words, and actions.

Zoroaster's teachings emphasize the responsibility of the wise to discern between these two spirits, aligning themselves with the force of good. This ethical dichotomy permeates the Persian religious framework, influencing how followers navigate their lives and engage with the divine.

While Ahriman falls short of the Lord in terms of dignity and power, his capacity to create and act independently underscores the perpetual struggle between these opposing cosmic forces. This struggle, far from an abstract concept, plays out in the choices and actions of individuals, echoing the eternal conflict between good and evil.

In essence, Zoroastrian dualism serves not only as a metaphysical understanding of the cosmos but also as a guide for ethical living. The call for wisdom in choosing the better path becomes a beacon for adherents to navigate the complexities of life, contributing to the shaping of a moral and conscientious society.

Ahura Mazda, the All-Knowing Lord, reveals himself through what is described as "the excellent, the pure and stirring word." In the rock inscription of Elvend commissioned by King Darius, these lines proclaim a monotheistic declaration:

"There is one God, omnipotent Ahura Mazda,
It is He who has created the earth here;
It is He who has created the heaven there;
It is He who has created mortal man."

Zoroaster's religious ethos shines through a common liturgical formula among the Persians. It serves as an introduction to worship and expresses a commitment to goodness and purity:

"May Ahura be rejoiced! May Angrô be destroyed by those who truly follow God's all-important will.

"I praise well-considered thoughts, well-spoken words, and well-done deeds. I embrace all good thoughts, good words, and good deeds; I reject all evil thoughts, evil words, and evil deeds.

"I give sacrifice and prayer unto you, O Ameshâ-Spentâ! With the fullness of my thoughts, my words, my deeds, and my heart: I give unto you even my own life.

"I recite the 'Praise of Holiness,' the Ashem Vohu:

"'Holiness is the best of all good. Well is it for it, well is it for that holiness which is perfection of holiness!

"'I confess myself a worshipper of Mazda, a follower of Zarathustra, one who hates the daêvas (devils) and obeys the laws of Ahura.'"

Lenormant describes Ahura Mazda as the creator, sovereign, and omniscient god, paralleling the Vedic god Varuna. The concept of the Supreme Being in the Avesta is presented as absolutely pure. The symbolic expressions, such as the sun as his eye or the heavens as his garment, are understood allegorically. Ahura Mazda is eternal, uncreated, and without end, having brought forth creation through the primal Word.

Regarding Ahriman, Lenormant depicts him as the perverter of the pure and perfect creation of Ahura Mazda. Ahriman, also known as the spirit of evil and the destroyer, engages in an eternal struggle with the god of order. The conflict between these two principles, good and evil, forms the crux of the world's history, drawing parallels to the Indo-Iranian myth of the serpent-demon Afrasiâb and the struggle in the atmosphere between the fire-god and the serpent-demon. This dualistic perspective, when generalized, laid the foundation for the establishment of dualism in Zoroastrianism.

In this religious framework, Zoroaster's teachings embody a commitment to a monotheistic faith, distinguishing Ahura Mazda as the supreme and benevolent creator. The emphasis on purity, goodness, and rejection of evil thoughts and deeds reflects a profound moral and ethical foundation. The liturgical formula serves as a testament to the Persian devotion to divine principles.

Ahura Mazda is not only the creator but also the sovereign ruler and omniscient deity, aligning with the Vedic god Varuna. The allegorical symbolism attributed to Ahura Mazda, such as the sun as his eye and the heavens as his garment, reinforces the purity and transcendence of this Supreme Being. His eternal existence, uncreated nature, and perpetual influence are underscored by the proclamation of the primal Word that initiated creation.

Conversely, Ahriman stands as the antagonist, disrupting the harmonious order created by Ahura Mazda. The perpetual struggle between these conflicting principles shapes the unfolding history of the world. The Indo-Iranian myth of Aji Dahâka, the serpent-demon attacking divine entities, finds resonance in the Greek myth of Apollo slaying the dragon Python.

In the words of James Darmesteter, the translator of the Zend-Avesta:

The Indo-Iranian religion rests on two fundamental ideas: the existence of a law in nature and an ongoing conflict within nature itself (Sacred Books of the East, IV., p. lvii).

The law in nature highlights the wisdom of Ahura, referred to as Mazda, the Wise. Simultaneously, the conflict in nature arises from the intrusion of Ahriman into Ahura's creation.

The fire sacrifice, accompanied by the consumption of the haoma drink, draws parallels to both the Vedic soma sacrifice in ancient India and the Christian Lord's Supper.

We learn from Persian sacred scriptures that consecrated cakes (draona) adorned with holy meat (myazda) were distributed among worshippers. More sacred, however, was the haoma drink, prepared from the white haoma plant or gaokerena, believed to confer immortality on the day of resurrection.

The Persian sacrament of drinking gaokerena, resembling Christian communion, finds historical echoes in early Christianity. Justinus notes that the solemnity of the Lord's Supper among Christians has similarities to the mysteries of Mithra, introduced by evil spirits.

After death, the Zoroastrian doctrine posits the soul's journey over the "accountant's bridge," cinvato pertush, where its fate is determined. The good traverse a broad path, while the wicked face peril. Intermediate souls, with balanced good and evil, await judgment until the great âka day.

A significant aspect of post-Zoroaster Persian religion centers on the anticipation of a transformative crisis, frashôkereti or frashakart, heralding the world's renewal. Saviors, born from Zoroaster's lineage, will emerge, culminating in the advent of the All-conquering Saviour, the "son of a virgin." This belief echoes in intensified forms during the days of John the Baptist and Jesus of Nazareth, proclaiming the imminent kingdom of heaven. The resurrection and transfiguration of the living and the dead are central themes in this eschatological vision.

The profound impact of Zoroaster's religion on Judaism and early Christianity is evident. The book of Ezra attributes the construction of the Lord's house in Jerusalem to Cyrus, the King, where eternal fire is worshipped. Jewish ceremonies also exhibit striking similarities to ancient Mazdaism rituals. Furthermore, "The Arabic Gospel of the Infancy" (Chapter 7) preserves evidence that Magi, following a prophecy of Zoroaster, journeyed from the East to Jerusalem.

This intersection of beliefs suggests a cross-cultural influence, with Zoroastrian ideas influencing the theological tapestry of both Judaism and early Christianity.

In Zoroastrianism, Ahura Mazda, the Omniscient Lord, communicates through the "excellent, the pure, and stirring word." A rock inscription commissioned by King Darius underscores the central role of Ahura Mazda as the creator of the earth, heaven, and mortal man.

The essence of Zoroaster's religion is encapsulated in liturgical worship, with invocations for the triumph over evil and adherence to divine will. Zoroastrians embrace virtuous thoughts, words, and deeds while rejecting their malevolent counterparts. Sacrifices and prayers are dedicated to Ameshâ-Spentâ, and a hymn, "Praise of Holiness," emphasizes the supremacy of holiness.

Zoroastrianism introduces the concept of cinvato pertush, the "accountant's bridge," representing the soul's journey after death. Depending on moral standing, individuals either face bliss or retribution. This eschatological framework culminates in the anticipation of frashôkereti, a crisis leading to the world's renewal. Saviors, born from Zoroaster's lineage, play pivotal roles in this transformative process, echoing themes later present in the Christian narrative.

The Zoroastrian sacrament of drinking gaokerena, akin to Christian communion, symbolizes spiritual rejuvenation and immortality. The Persian belief in a savior reflects the messianic expectations mirrored in early Christianity, as illustrated by the resurrection and transfiguration narratives.

The profound impact of Zoroaster's teachings on Judaism and early Christianity underscores the intricate tapestry of religious evolution. The echoes of Zoroastrian concepts in various religious practices highlight the interconnectedness of ancient belief systems and their enduring influence on subsequent faith traditions.

In the Judaic context, the book of Ezra explicitly credits King Cyrus with building the house of the Lord in Jerusalem, where worship is conducted "with the eternal fire." This reference implies a direct connection between Persian and Judaic religious practices. Furthermore, the persistence of certain Jewish rituals with parallels in Mazdaism suggests an ongoing cultural exchange.

The story of the Magi in "The Arabic Gospel of the Infancy" strengthens the ties between Zoroastrianism and early Christianity. The Magi, considered Zoroastrian priests, are portrayed as coming from the East to Jerusalem based on a prophecy attributed to Zoroaster. This narrative aligns with the biblical account of the Magi visiting the infant Jesus, indicating a shared prophetic expectation transcending religious boundaries.

The anticipation of a savior figure in both Zoroastrianism and early Christianity, born of divine lineage and bringing about spiritual transformation, underscores a common theme. The concept of resurrection, the transfiguration of bodies, and the expectation of a messianic era bear resemblance across these traditions.

The fluid exchange of religious ideas, symbols, and rituals among ancient cultures illustrates a dynamic interplay of beliefs, fostering a shared spiritual heritage. Zoroastrianism's influence on Judaism and early Christianity exemplifies the intricate web of cultural and religious interconnectedness, shaping the collective spiritual imagination of humanity across different epochs.

The Persian worldview, much like the religion of the Jews, lacked the concrete imagery that would stimulate artistic expression. Consequently, we lack distinct depictions of spirits, whether benevolent or malevolent, that can be uniquely attributed to Persian culture. Even representations of Ahura Mazda, the god of light and goodness, found in various bas-reliefs, do not originate from an independently recognized concept. The figure representing the deity rising from the bust has connections to Assyrian emblems and could potentially trace its roots to Accadian origins. An Assyrian cylinder, for instance, depicts a worshipper in front of a god's idol with the tree of life and a priest carrying a rosary, much resembling the Ahura Mazda depictions in Persian art.

Ahura Mazda is portrayed as a winged disc without a head, resembling Chaldean sun-pictures, as seen in a cameo depicting him being worshipped by two sphinxes alongside the sacred haoma plant. Another cameo portrays him as a human figure without wings emerging from a hovering crescent above a sacrificial fire. The sun is depicted above him, and a priest or king stands in adoration before him. The absence of exclusively Persian representations further emphasizes the abstract nature of Persian religious concepts, limiting distinctive artistic developments.

The abstract nature of Persian religious concepts, shared with the Jewish faith, hindered the development of distinctive artistic representations. This absence is notable in the depictions of both benevolent and malevolent spirits, which lack unique Persian characteristics. Even the representations of Ahura Mazda, the god of light and goodness, seem to draw influence from Assyrian emblems, possibly with roots in Accadian origins.

In various bas-reliefs, Ahura Mazda's figure rising from a bust shares similarities with an Assyrian cylinder depicting a worshipper before a god's idol, flanked by the tree of life and a priest with a rosary. This echoes the imagery found in Persian art depicting Ahura Mazda.

Depictions of Ahura Mazda vary, with some portraying him as a winged disc without a head, reminiscent of Chaldean sun-pictures. In one cameo, he is worshipped by sphinxes beside the sacred haoma plant. Another cameo portrays him as a human figure without wings emerging from a hovering crescent above a sacrificial fire. Above him, the sun is depicted, and a priest or king stands in adoration.

The lack of unique Persian depictions underscores the abstract nature of their religious beliefs, which may not have lent themselves to the development of specific artistic representations.

Ancient Persian monuments feature magnificent representations of Ahura Mazda, drawing attention with a lofty and majestic presence that surpasses Assyrian concepts of deities. In these depictions, Ahura Mazda holds either a ring or the short royal staff, resembling a lotus flower at the top.

According to Prof. A. V. Williams Jackson, the ring symbolizes the "Circle of Sovereignty," while the loop with streamers is interpreted as a variation of the same idea. It appears as a chaplet or waist-garland with ribbons in some representations. The loop with streamers is not considered to be a disc representing the sun, unlike similar Assyrian sculptures that unequivocally depict the sun.

Although no representation of Ahriman has been found among Persian antiquities, a Persepolis bas-relief shows the king slaying a unicorn, resembling the Assyrian Tiamat. This suggests that the Persian sculptor emulated the style of Assyrian predecessors.

The origin of Zoroaster's dualism has limited information, but remnants of Devil-worship persist in a sect known as the Izedis, considered fossil representatives of pre-Zoroastrian beliefs. This sect, still existing in Mesopotamia, has a peculiar form of dualism, giving special reverence to Satan. The Izedis' beliefs align with the Persian origin of their religion, combining Christian and Islamic elements with remnants of Devil-worship.

The evolution of Persian religion involved a transition from Devil-worship of the daêvas, deities of natural forces, to a higher form of God-worship. The recognition of moral power, embodied in virtues like the Ameshâ Spentâ, marked a significant shift, propelling Persia to become a leading nation in the ancient world. This transformative change represented a crucial step forward in their religious and cultural development.

The Persian worldview, akin to the Jewish religion, was too abstract to encourage significant artistic development. Consequently, there are no exclusive and distinctive representations of either good or evil spirits in Persian art. Even depictions of Ahura Mazda, the god of light and goodness, do not originate from an original Persian conception. The figure, seen on various bas-reliefs, can be traced back to Assyrian emblems and might even have Accadian origins. One such Assyrian cylinder portrays a worshipper in front of a god with the tree of life behind them, similar to Persian depictions of Ahura Mazda.

Ahura Mazda is often represented as a winged disc without a head, reminiscent of Chaldean sun-pictures, or as a human figure without wings, rising from a crescent hovering above the sacrificial fire. The loop with streamers is interpreted differently, sometimes as the "Circle of Sovereignty," and its origin is distinct from the disc representing the sun in Egyptian temple decorations. Assyrian sculptures featuring a winged disc with feather-tail and streamers also depict the sun in various mythological contexts.

While representations of Ahura Mazda exist on Persian monuments, there is no known depiction of Ahriman. However, a bas-relief in Persepolis shows the king slaying a unicorn, resembling the Assyrian Tiamat. This suggests a continuation of the stylistic influence of Assyrian art in Persian sculpture.

The Izedis, a sect known as Devil-worshippers, serve as contemporary remnants of pre-Zoroastrian beliefs. Their peculiar form of dualism involves recognizing a Supreme Being while offering peculiar reverence to Satan, chief of the angelic host. The Izedis' beliefs align with a Persian origin, hinting at a historical connection between their creed and ancient Persian Devil-worship.

The Persian religion underwent a significant evolution, transitioning from Devil-worship of the daêvas, representing natural forces, to a higher form of God-worship. The recognition of moral power, embodied in virtues like the Ameshâ Spentâ, was a pivotal development that propelled Persia into becoming a major cultural and religious force in the ancient world. This transformation marked a crucial step forward in their religious and cultural evolution.

The Persians, in prehistoric times, likely shared similarities with groups like the Izedis, practicing a form of Devil-worship focused on appeasing the daêvas, deities representing natural forces. Sacrifices were made to these irresistible forces, reflecting a belief system devoid of a comprehensive understanding of moral virtues. Over time, a profound shift occurred in Persian religious consciousness, marked by the ascendancy of God-worship over Devil-worship.

This transformation is evident in the emergence of Zoroastrianism, with its foundational figure, Zoroaster, advocating a radical departure from the older practices. The recognition of moral virtues, personified in the Ameshâ Spentâ, signaled a profound evolution in Persian spirituality. While the Izedis remained entrenched in their peculiar dualism, Zoroaster ushered in an era where moral endeavor and the pursuit of goodness gained paramount importance.

As the Persians embraced a higher understanding of divinity, their cultural and religious identity underwent a remarkable shift. The transition from Devil-worship to God-worship marked a pivotal moment in their history. The subsequent development of Zoroastrianism, with its emphasis on moral principles and a singular divine entity, contributed to the rise of Persia as a prominent and influential civilization in the ancient world. This metamorphosis laid the foundation for a distinctive Persian identity, setting them on a trajectory that would shape their role in the broader cultural landscape.

Zoroastrianism, under the influence of Zoroaster's teachings, became a unifying force for the Persians. The religion emphasized the cosmic battle between the forces of good, represented by Ahura Mazda, and the forces of evil, embodied by Ahriman. This dualistic framework provided a moral and spiritual foundation for Persian society.

Zoroaster's doctrines, captured in the Gathas, portrayed

him not as a demigod but as a human prophet with a message of ethical responsibility and devotion to Ahura Mazda. The Persian people, once torn between the worship of daêvas and the reverence for Ahura, rallied behind Zoroaster's vision of a higher, more ethical deity.

The impact of Zoroastrianism extended beyond religious beliefs, influencing Persian culture, governance, and social norms. The adoption of the "Circle of Sovereignty" as a symbol of Ahura Mazda's dominion reflected a fusion of religious and political ideals. The emphasis on moral choices and adherence to the divine order shaped Persian ethics.

The Persian religion's evolution is also mirrored in the anticipation of a great renewal, frashôkereti, reflecting a belief in a future savior and a resurrection of the dead. This eschatological outlook resonated with later messianic expectations, influencing Judaism and early Christianity.

The cultural legacy of Zoroastrianism persists in the echoes of its dualism, moral teachings, and concepts of divine justice. The transition from Devil-worship to God-worship, driven by the teachings of Zoroaster, left an indelible mark on the Persian identity, contributing to their rise as a civilization of significance in the ancient world.

The legacy of Zoroastrianism in shaping the Persian identity is also evident in the realm of art and symbolism. While the religion's abstract nature did not lend itself to extensive artistic representations, the images of Ahura Mazda on Persian monuments display a distinct loftiness and majesty, distinguishing them from the more anthropomorphic deities of Assyrian art.

The representations of Ahura Mazda holding a ring or a

royal staff, often resembling a lotus flower, embody the concept of the "Circle of Sovereignty." This symbolism, along with the loop and streamers, is interpreted as a visual representation of divine authority. While the origins of these symbols are complex, their recurrence in various contexts, such as sun depictions in Assyrian art, suggests a shared cultural language.

Conversely, artistic representations of Ahriman are less prevalent among Persian antiquities. A bas-relief in Persepolis depicting the king slaying a unicorn draws parallels to Assyrian motifs, highlighting the influence of earlier artistic traditions on Persian sculptors.

The dualistic elements in Zoroastrianism find echoes in the Izedis, a sect preserving remnants of Devil-worship in Mesopotamia. This continuity suggests that Zoroaster's dualism may have evolved from earlier beliefs in the daêvas. The Izedis' peculiar dualistic creed, with a focus on Satan as a potential benefactor, mirrors the transition from primitive Devil-worship to a more nuanced understanding of cosmic forces.

Ultimately, Zoroastrianism's evolution from a primitive form of Devil-worship to a more refined system of God-worship played a crucial role in shaping the Persian worldview. The ethical framework, religious symbolism, and eschatological beliefs propagated by Zoroaster left an enduring imprint on Persian culture, influencing subsequent civilizations and contributing to the rich tapestry of ancient history.

Footnotes

- Journal of the American Oriental Society, Vol. XVII., p. 96.

- In a letter to Professor Jackson alluded to on page 20 of his essay.

- The story that Croesus's life was saved through Zoroastrian influences upon the mind of Cyrus, as told by Nicolaus Damascenus who wrote in the first century B. C., is quite probable. We read (in fragm. 65, Müller, Fragm. Hist. Gr., iii., 409) that religious scruples rose in addition to other considerations, and the words of Zoroaster (Ζωροάστρου λόγια) were called to mind that the fire should not be defiled. Therefore the Persians shouted that the life of Croesus should be spared. Compare Harlez, Avesta traduit, Introd., pp. xliv., lxvii.

- Druj, fiend, is always feminine, while Ahriman is masculine.

- The Turanian form of Afrasiâb, was probably Farrusarrabba.

- Compare Sacred Books of the East, XXXI., p. 29.

- "The creative Word which was in the beginning" (Ahuna-Vairyo, Honover) reminds one not only of the Christian idea of the λόγος ὁς ἦν ἐν ἀρχή, but also of the Brahman Vâch (word, etymologically the same as the Latin vox), which is glorified in the fourth hymn of the Rig Vêda, as "pervading heaven and earth, existing in all the worlds and extending to the heavens."

- Translated from Lenormant's French rendering, 1. c., p. 388.

- Cf. Sacred Books of the East, Vol. XXIII., p. 22.

- The six Ameshâ-Spentâ (the undying and well-doing ones) are what Christians might call archangels. Originally they had been seven, but the first and greatest among them, Ahura Mazda, came to overshadow the divinity of the other six. They remained powerful gods, but he was regarded as their father arid creator. We read in Yast, XIX., 16, that they have "one and the same thinking, one and the same speaking, one and the same doing, one and the same father and lord, who is Ahura Mazda."

At first the Ameshâ Spentâ were mere personifications of virtues, but later on they were entrusted with the government of the various domains of the universe. Haurvatât and Ameretât (health and immortality) had charge of waters and trees. Khshathrem Vairîm (perfect sovereignty), represented the flash of lightning. His emblem being molten brass, he was revered as the master of metals. Asha Vahita (excellent holiness), the moral world-order as symbolised by sacrifice and burnt-offering, ruled over the fire. Spenta Armaití (divine piety) continued to be regarded as the goddess of the earth, which position, according to old traditions, she had held since the Indo-Iranian era; and Vohu Manô (good thought) superintended the creation of animate life. (See Darmesteter, Ormuzd et Ahriman, Paris: 1877. pp. 55, 202-206. Comp. Encyclopædia Britannica, s. v. "Zoroaster," and Sacred Books of the East, Vol. IV., p. LXXI., et seq.) For an exposition of the modern Parseeism of India see Mr. Dosabhai Framji Karaka's History of the Parsis, London, 1884.

- Says Darmesteter: "The 'Ashem Vohu' is one of the holiest and most frequently recited prayers."

- For a concise statement of the Persian religion, which in many respects foreshadows the Christian doctrines of a Saviour and of the bodily resurrection of the dead, see Prof. A. V. Williams Jackson's excellent article, "The Ancient Persian Doctrine of a Future Life," published in the Biblical World, August, 1896.

- See his article on "The Circle of Sovereignty," in the American Oriental Society's Proceedings, May, 1889.

- See K. O. Kiash, Ancient Persian Sculptures; and also Rawlinson, J. R. A. S., X.. p. 187. Kossowicz, Inscriptiones Palaeo Persicae Achaemeniodorum, P. 46 et seq.

- There is no need of enumerating other cylinders and bas-reliefs of the same kind, as they are too frequently found in Assyrian archæology. See for instance the illustrations in Lenormant, 1. 1. V., pp. 177, 230, 247, 296, 299, etc.

6

ISRAEL

Azazel, the God of the Desert

The early phases of Hebrew civilization remain somewhat obscure when it comes to describing the evolution of the Israelite concept of God before it reached the purity of the Yahveh (Yahweh) conception. Although not well-documented, it appears that the Israelites might have had a deity resembling the Egyptian Typhon. An indication of this lies in the practice of sacrificing a goat to Azazel, considered the demon of the desert, pointing to a time when the Israelites were transitioning from a dualistic worldview where both principles were seen as equal.

In Leviticus 16, it is stated:

"Aaron shall cast lots upon the two goats; one for the Lord, and the other for Azazel. Aaron shall bring the goat upon which the Lord's lot fell and offer him for a sin-offering. But the goat on which the lot fell for Azazel shall be presented alive before the Lord, to make atonement with him and to let him go to Azazel in the desert."

The name Azazel is derived from "aziz," meaning strength, and "El," meaning God. The god of war at Edessa is referred to as Asisos, the strong one. Bal-aziz was the strong god, and Rosh-aziz, the head of the strong one, is the name of a promontory on the Phoenician coast. Therefore, Azazel signifies the Strength of God.

The mention of Azazel reflects a remnant of prior dualism. Azazel, the god of the desert, transitioned from being the strong god to a mere shadow of his former power, as the scapegoat is no longer sacrificed. Only Yahveh's goat is offered for a sin-offering, while the scapegoat carries the curse of the people's sin into the desert. Thus, the worship of Azazel evolved into a mere acknowledgment of his existence. These sacrificial rituals, remnants of an older dualism, linger in Hebrew literature, portraying a time when the power of evil received equal worship with the power of good.

Superstitions

While the Old Testament contains many noble ideas and profound truths, it is an extraordinary collection of religious books, highly esteemed in the world's literature. Nevertheless, amidst the valuable content, there are instances of confusion and regrettable errors that were, surprisingly, considered essential aspects of the Israelite religion by some of its leaders. The Bible authors not only attributed crimes committed by their own people, such as theft (Exodus 11) and murder and rape (Numbers 31:17-18), to God but also endorsed superstitious practices reminiscent of those common among primitive societies.

One such sanctioned practice was the burial of people alive under foundation stones. According to biblical accounts, when God commanded the destruction of Jericho, all its inhabitants, men, women, young and old, along with livestock, were slain, except Rahab, a woman with a questionable reputation who had sided with the enemies of her people. Joshua, in response, issued a curse:

"Cursed be the man before the Lord, that riseth up and buildeth this city Jericho: he shall lay the foundation thereof in his first born and in his youngest son shall he set up the gates of it."

Despite the curse, Jericho was bound to be rebuilt due to its strategic significance as the key to Palestine and the gateway from the desert. The man who took on this task, Hiel the Bethelite, was superstitious enough to fulfill Joshua's curse. In the Book of Kings (1 Kings 16:34), during the reign of Ahab, it is stated:

"In his days, Hiel the Bethelite built Jericho; he laid the foundation stones thereof in Abiram, his firstborn, and set up the gates thereof in his youngest son, Segub, according to the word of the Lord which he spake by Joshua, the son of Nun."

Additionally, the witch prosecutions during the Middle Ages in Christianity find their roots in passages from the Old Testament.

These prosecutions were influenced by biblical passages that fueled fear and suspicion regarding witchcraft. One notable example is Exodus 22:18, which states, "You shall not permit a sorceress to live." This verse contributed to a climate where individuals accused of practicing witchcraft were subject to persecution and often faced severe consequences.

The Old Testament, while containing profound moral teachings and ethical guidelines, also reflects the cultural and historical context of its time. The persistence of superstitious beliefs and harsh practices in certain passages reveals the evolving nature of religious thought and the challenges of interpreting ancient texts in a contemporary context. It underscores the importance of critical examination and contextual understanding when approaching religious scriptures.

In the laws of Exodus (Exodus 22:18), there is a provision for capital punishment in cases of witchcraft. The same command is reiterated in Leviticus, stating that those who turn to familiar spirits and wizards will face severe consequences, including being cut off from their people. The punishment is described as stoning, and the severity of these laws is evident.

Despite the strict regulations against wizards and witches, the Israelites often sought their help. King Saul, who had previously tried to eliminate soothsayers, turned to the witch of Endor in a moment of great anxiety.

Various passages suggest that the Israelites believed in

evil spirits inhabiting dark and desolate places. These spirits had names such as Seirim (goat-spirits), Lilith (the nightly one), and Shedim (demons). The Seirim are reminiscent of Assyrian depictions of evil spirits in the form of goats.

The existence of these demons in Hebrew beliefs raises questions about whether they represent remnants of an earlier, less monotheistic religious stage or simply reflect the enduring superstitions of the time.

As a purer religion gradually emerged, traces of devil-worship, including bestial rites and human sacrifices, persisted. Even as a more radiant light began to shine in the world, the habits of a primitive age lingered.

The transition from Azazel to Satan marked a shift from the belief in a God of Evil to the concept of an evil demon. Satan, associated with temptation and the origin of all evil, became linked with the serpent from the Genesis story.

While the term "Satan" is rarely mentioned in the Old Testament as a proper name for the Devil, the concept of an enemy or adversary (Satan in its literal sense) is more frequently used. Notably, the same event is attributed to both Yahveh and Satan in different passages, highlighting the evolving nature of these religious beliefs.

The gradual shift from Azazel to Satan represents a change in the conceptualization of evil forces. Azazel, once considered the Strength of God, faded into a shadow of its former power, eventually replaced by the figure of Satan. This transformation marked a departure from the earlier dualistic beliefs, where both principles of good and evil were considered equal.

The Old Testament, despite containing noble ideas and

great truths, also harbored lamentable errors and superstitions. Certain laws and practices, such as the ritual of sacrificing a goat to Azazel, hinted at the Israelites' lingering connection to dualistic beliefs.

The severe laws against wizards and witches coexisted with the Israelites' inclination to seek their help in times of trouble. Even King Saul, who had previously condemned soothsayers, resorted to consulting the witch of Endor during moments of anxiety.

The Hebrew beliefs in evil spirits dwelling in dark places, such as Seirim, Lilith, and Shedim, may have roots in earlier religious stages or simply reflected the prevalent superstitions of the time. The Assyrian depictions of goat demons provide parallels to the Seirim in Hebrew beliefs.

The emergence of a purer religion was a slow process, and vestiges of devil-worship and its associated rites endured, including human sacrifices. The transition from Azazel to Satan signifies the evolving nature of religious beliefs and the replacement of the God of Evil with the concept of a malevolent adversary.

While the term "Satan" is infrequently used in the Old Testament as a proper name for the Devil, the idea of an adversary or enemy (Satan in its literal sense) is more commonly employed. The attribution of the same event to both Yahveh and Satan in different passages underscores the dynamic nature of these evolving religious narratives.

In 2 Samuel 24:1, it is mentioned:

"The Lord became angry with Israel, and He moved David to say, 'Go, number Israel and Judah.'"

The same incident is recounted in 1 Chronicles 21:1:

"Satan stood up against Israel and incited David to number Israel."

In the earlier Hebrew texts, particularly in the Pentateuch, Satan is entirely absent. Punishments, revenge, and temptations are all attributed to Yahveh or His angel following His explicit command. Events like the temptation of Abraham, the plague on the firstborn in Egypt, the destruction of Sodom and Gomorrah with brimstone and fire, the harmful spirit that afflicted Saul, and the pestilence sent to punish David are directly ascribed to God. Even instances like the misleading spirit among the Egyptians (Isaiah 19:14), the lying spirit in the mouths of Ahab's prophets (1 Kings 22:23, also 2 Chronicles 18:20-22), and instances of ignorance and indifference (Isaiah 29:10) are explicitly linked to God's actions.

The prophet Zechariah describes Satan as an angel whose role is to accuse and demand the punishment of the wicked. In the Book of Job, where a vivid portrayal of the Evil One is presented, Satan emerges as a malicious servant of God, reveling in the roles of tempter, tormentor, and avenger. His accusations are unjust, resembling a prosecutor's habitual pursuit of charges, and he takes pleasure in convicting even the innocent. However, there is no questioning of God's justice and goodness in this narrative.

Interestingly, in the canonical Old Testament books, Satan is portrayed as an adversary of humanity, not God. He is considered a subject of God and a faithful servant of the divine will.

The Jewish concept of Satan gained additional attributes from the characteristics of gods in neighboring nations. Throughout history, the deities of opposing nations often transformed into evil spirits. Beelzebub, the Phoenician god, evolved into another name for Satan, while Hinnom, associated with the worship of Moloch, became the Hebrew term for hell, replacing Sheol, the underworld for the deceased. The idol of Moloch, made of brass with a furnace for a stomach, was used to sacrifice children, according to prophets. This grim practice was denounced by King Josiah, who sought to eradicate it by defiling Tophet in the valley of the children of Hinnom (2 Kings 23:10). The name of this foreign deity, due to its association with abominable practices, naturally became a symbol of detestation and diabolical superstition among the Israelites.

In 2 Samuel 24:1, the text reveals:

"The Lord became angry with Israel, and He influenced David to say, 'Go, number Israel and Judah.'"

A similar incident is recorded in 1 Chronicles 21:1:

"Satan stood against Israel and incited David to count Israel."

The earlier Hebrew texts, particularly in the Pentateuch, make no mention of Satan. Acts of punishment, revenge, and temptation are explicitly attributed to Yahveh or His angel following His direct command. Instances such as the temptation of Abraham, the plague on Egypt's firstborn, the destruction of Sodom and Gomorrah with brimstone and fire, the harmful spirit afflicting Saul, and the pestilence sent to punish David are all ascribed directly to God. Even events like the misleading spirit among the Egyptians (Isaiah 19:14), the lying spirit in the mouths of Ahab's prophets (1 Kings 22:23, also 2 Chronicles 18:20-22), and instances of ignorance and indifference (Isaiah 29:10) are explicitly linked to God's actions.

The prophet Zechariah portrays Satan as an angel whose role is to accuse and demand punishment for the wicked. In the Book of Job, where an intricate picture of the Evil One is presented, Satan appears as a malicious servant of God, delighting in the roles of tempter, tormentor, and avenger. His accusations are unjust, reminiscent of a prosecutor habitually pursuing charges, and he takes pleasure in convicting even the innocent. Yet, in this narrative, there is no questioning of God's justice and goodness.

Notably, in the canonical Old Testament books, Satan is depicted as an adversary of humanity rather than God. He is seen as a subject of God and a faithful servant of the divine will.

The Jewish notion of Satan acquired additional attributes from the characteristics of gods in neighboring nations. Throughout history, the deities of opposing nations often transformed into evil spirits. Beelzebub, the Phoenician god, evolved into another name for Satan, while Hinnom, linked to the worship of Moloch, became the Hebrew term for hell, replacing Sheol, the underworld for the deceased. The idol of Moloch, made of brass with a furnace for a stomach, was used to sacrifice children, according to the prophets. King Josiah denounced this grim practice and sought to eradicate it by defiling Tophet in the valley of the children of Hinnom (2 Kings 23:10). The name of this foreign deity, due to its association with abominable practices, naturally became a symbol of detestation and diabolical superstition among the Israelites.

In the subsequent centuries, the concept of Satan continued to evolve within Jewish thought. By the time of the Second Temple period, Satan had taken on a more distinct identity as an accuser and adversary. The Book of Enoch, a collection of apocalyptic literature, further developed the figure of Satan as a rebellious angel who leads a group of fallen angels in opposition to God.

During the post-exilic period, Judaism encountered various influences from Persian, Hellenistic, and Roman cultures. These external factors contributed to the shaping of Jewish beliefs, and Satan became more prominent in apocalyptic and mystical traditions. The idea of a cosmic battle between the forces of good and evil gained traction, with Satan assuming the role of the chief antagonist.

By the time of Jesus and the emergence of early Christianity, Satan had become a central figure in Jewish apocalyptic thought. The New Testament incorporates and expands upon these ideas, presenting Satan as a tempter, the ruler of demons, and an adversary to both God and humanity. The Gospels recount episodes where Jesus confronts and overcomes the temptations of Satan, reinforcing the cosmic struggle between good and evil.

The evolution of the Satan figure in Jewish and early Christian literature demonstrates the dynamic nature of religious concepts and their adaptation to changing cultural and theological landscapes. As Judaism and Christianity developed, so did their understanding of the supernatural realm, including the role of Satan as a malevolent force opposed to divine purposes.

As Christianity continued to spread and establish itself as

a distinct religious tradition, the portrayal of Satan underwent further developments. Early Christian theologians, influenced by Jewish apocalypticism and Hellenistic thought, began to elaborate on the nature of Satan and his role in the cosmic drama.

In Christian theology, Satan became associated with the fallen angel Lucifer, who rebelled against God and was cast out of heaven. This narrative is not explicitly detailed in the Bible but draws on interpretative traditions and later writings. The biblical passages that mentioned the fall of Satan (such as Isaiah 14:12-15 and Ezekiel 28:12-19) were often allegorically linked to the devil's rebellion.

During the medieval period, Christian theology and art further solidified the image of Satan as a horned, cloven-hoofed, and malevolent being. The idea of hell as a realm ruled by Satan gained prominence, and depictions of the Last Judgment often featured Satan tormenting the damned.

The concept of witchcraft and demonic pacts also became intertwined with the figure of Satan during the Middle Ages. The witch trials of the Early Modern period saw an upsurge in accusations of individuals making pacts with the devil and engaging in malevolent magic.

In the context of the Protestant Reformation, various reformers, such as Martin Luther and John Calvin, emphasized the reality of Satan and demonic forces. The devil became a convenient figure to blame for societal upheavals, plagues, and other calamities.

Throughout the centuries, the image of Satan has continued to evolve within Christian traditions. Some contemporary Christian denominations interpret Satan metaphorically or focus more on the internal struggle against sin. Others maintain a more literal understanding of Satan as a supernatural being actively opposing God and seeking to lead humanity astray. The complexity of Satan's character remains a topic of theological reflection and interpretation within Christian theology.

Understanding the historical connection between Israel's religion and the mythologies of Assyria and Babylon has become clearer with the deciphering of ancient cuneiform records. Significant remnants of Bel Merodach's battle with Tiamat can be found in the Old Testament. Hermann Gunkel, after providing a literal translation of various passages with explanatory comments, notes:

"While the actual narrative of Yahveh's combat with the dragon is not explicitly recounted in existing literature, the Old Testament contains many references presupposing the myth. Judaism, focused on compiling the canon, avoided incorporating myths reminiscent of paganism. However, the absence of the dragon myth in the canon, which need not be lamented from the perspective of Christian readers, serves as clear evidence that our Old Testament is just a fragment of the extensive old religious literature."

"The myth, from its inception in Israel, was a hymn to Yahveh. Consequently, references to the dragon myth are commonly made in Yahveh-hymns, as seen in Psalm lxxxix. Various Old Testament passages, whether depicting Yahveh's oppression of humanity, emphasizing Yahveh's omnipotence, or inspiring hope in a people under foreign rule, directly acknowledge Yahveh's power over the dragon."

"It is interesting to note that the seven-armed candlestick

on the arch of Titus features dragon figures on its base, likely representing Leviathan, Behemoth, and Rahab—the mythological monsters of Israel."

These dragon figures, presumably representing Leviathan, Behemoth, and Rahab, are depicted on the base of the seven-armed candlestick found on the arch of Titus. This symbolism aligns with the rich mythological heritage of Israel, as these monsters played significant roles in the narratives of Yahveh's power and dominance.

Although the Old Testament does not explicitly narrate the myth of Yahveh's combat with the dragon, references to this myth are embedded in various passages. Notably, Psalm lxxxix stands out as a beautiful instance where the Yahveh-hymn intertwines with the dragon myth, portraying Yahveh's oppression of humanity.

The absence of the dragon myth from the canon, due to Judaism's deliberate exclusion of pagan-scented myths, indicates that the Old Testament we possess is just a fragment of the broader religious literature. Despite this omission, the myth remained well-known and popular among the people, evident in its implicit presence throughout the Old Testament.

Scholars recognize that these dragon references highlight the enduring influence of the myth on Israel's religious consciousness. Whether employed by poets, prophets, or those inspiring hope in times of adversity, direct allusions to Yahveh's power over the dragon persist as a powerful motif in the Old Testament. This underscores the profound impact of mythological elements on the religious and cultural tapestry of ancient Israel.

As we explore the historical connections between Israel's religion and the mythologies of Assyria and Babylon, the deciphering of ancient cuneiform records sheds light on the rich tapestry of influences. Reminiscences of Bel Merodach's legendary battle with Tiamat, a dragon-like entity, are subtly woven into the Old Testament.

While the canon of Judaism deliberately refrains from narrating the myth of Yahveh's combat with the dragon, it is evident that this myth was deeply ingrained in the cultural fabric. The absence of a direct portrayal in the canon, an intentional choice to distance from heathen influences, underscores the selectivity of the Old Testament we have today. It is a mere fragment of a more expansive religious literature that once existed.

The myth, a hymn to Yahveh from Israel's inception, finds indirect but profound expression in the Yahveh-hymn. Psalm lxxxix is a notable example where this theme is beautifully intertwined with Yahveh's oppression of humanity. Poets, prophets, and those inspiring hope during trying times consistently allude to Yahveh's power over the dragon, emphasizing its enduring significance.

Remarkably, artifacts like the seven-armed candlestick on the arch of Titus depict figures assumed to represent Leviathan, Behemoth, and Rahab—mythological monsters that hold key roles in Israel's narratives. This visual representation aligns with the symbolic importance of these creatures in Israel's cultural and religious imagination.

As our understanding of ancient cuneiform records deepens, we unveil the intricate historical connection between Israel's religious narratives and the mythologies of Assyria and Babylon. Notably, remnants of the epic clash between Bel Merodach and Tiamat resonate in the Old Testament, subtly alluded to rather than explicitly recounted.

The deliberate omission of the dragon-slaying myth from the canon of Judaism, likely due to its associations with heathen traditions, highlights the selective nature of the Old Testament we possess. It stands as a curated fragment, hinting at a more extensive religious literature that once flourished. The absence of direct narration, especially within the Yahveh-hymn, serves as an implicit acknowledgment of the myth's prevalence and popularity among the people.

Psalm lxxxix emerges as a poignant illustration of how the myth seamlessly intersects with Yahveh's oppression of humanity. Poets, prophets, and leaders, whether inspiring hope or underscoring divine omnipotence, consistently reference Yahveh's supremacy over the dragon. This indirect yet pervasive integration underscores the enduring importance of the myth within Israel's cultural and religious tapestry.

Intriguingly, visual artifacts like the seven-armed candlestick on the arch of Titus contribute to this narrative, featuring figures assumed to depict Leviathan, Behemoth, and Rahab—mythological monsters intricately woven into Israel's stories. These symbolic representations further affirm the mythical legacy that transcends textual confines.

Footnotes

1. It is entirely reasonable to accept the Biblical accounts regarding Moloch, as Diodorus (20, 14) corroborates the description of the cult surrounding the national god of Carthage,

whom he equates with the Greek deity "Kronos." Considering that Carthage is a Phoenician colony, there are compelling grounds to identify this Kronos with the Ammonite Moloch, both appeased by similarly horrifying sacrifices.

2. The passages in question become significantly clearer when interpreted through the lens provided by Gunkel. Without such guidance, these references remain cryptic to readers, as the translations in our Bible do little to aid their comprehension.

7

BRAHMANISM AND HINDUISM

India, the ancient cradle of religion and philosophy, exhibits a strong inclination towards monism, contrasting with the Persian affinity for dualism. However, India's early monism often drifts into pantheism, where the absolute, or the concept of the All, is considered real, while all concrete existences are viewed as mere illusions or dreams.

In popular Hinduism, which embraces polytheism, there's a practical pantheism where various deities are seen as facets of the One and All, blurring distinctions between good and evil. The cosmic struggle between these forces is seen as a cycle of divine incarnations, necessitated by issues like tyranny, injustice, disrespect for priests, or disruptions caused by the warrior caste.

The gods in Hinduism, despite their benevolence, are not

purely good, often assuming forms that might seem demonic in Western eyes. The same deities embody both life-affirming and destructive aspects.

Brahma, the highest god in Brahmanism, symbolizes the All or the abstract concept of being. The Trimurti, a trinity comprising Brahma, Vishnu, and Siva, represents the diverse aspects of the divine.

Brahma, the originator of all beings, is the divine mind and father of the universes. He emerges from undifferentiated being and is associated with Sarasvati, the goddess of poetry, learning, and music. Brahma, in the Yajurveda, is described as the creator of man, producing the soul from himself and clothing it with a body, a process presented in reverse order in the Hebrew Genesis.

Vishnu, another member of the Trimurti, plays a crucial role as the preserver and protector of the universe. He intervenes through various incarnations, or avatars, whenever cosmic order is disrupted. His well-known avatars include Krishna and Rama.

Siva, the third deity in the Trimurti, embodies the destructive force but also plays a crucial role in regeneration and renewal. He is often depicted as Nataraja, the cosmic dancer, symbolizing the cyclical nature of creation, preservation, and destruction.

The Brahmanic gods are not limited to benevolent aspects; they also possess destructive qualities, emphasizing the intricate balance in Hindu cosmology. The gods and goddesses are revered for their various attributes, reflecting the multifaceted nature of existence.

It's essential to note that Hindu cosmology, with its rich

tapestry of deities and their diverse attributes, may seem complex and paradoxical. The underlying theme, however, emphasizes the interconnectedness of all things and the cyclical nature of existence, reinforcing the notion of the eternal and ever-changing reality.

As we explore Hindu cosmology, we find a fascinating blend of monism, pantheism, and the intricate dance of deities, reflecting the diverse spiritual traditions that have evolved in the vast and ancient tapestry of Indian philosophy and religion.

Brahma, often depicted with four heads and hands holding symbolic items, occupies a significant place in philosophical discussions, representing the life-breath of the world, known as Atman. In popular worship, however, Brahma has not gained as much prominence as Vishnu, the second member of the trinity.

Vishnu, a key deity associated with avatars or incarnations, holds practical importance for the people. His ten incarnations include the Matsya-Avatar, where he takes the form of a fish to retrieve stolen Vedas during a deluge. This event intriguingly parallels a theme in the gnostic Pistis Sophia, linking it to the preservation of sacred texts.

In the Kurm-Avatar, Vishnu transforms into a tortoise to support the world-pillar, Mandaras mountain, and the world-serpent, Vasuki, during the churning of the ocean. This cosmic event yields valuable treasures, including Vishnu's gem, Kaustubha, and various divine beings such as Apsaras, Indra's horse, and Kamadhenu, the cow of plenty.

The Varaha-Avatar portrays Vishnu as a wild boar, rescuing the earth submerged in the cosmic ocean. The

Narasimha-Avatar features Vishnu as a man-lion, defeating the demon Hiranyakashipu and restoring cosmic balance.

These vivid narratives highlight the dynamic and diverse nature of Hindu mythology, emphasizing the symbolic significance and practical relevance of Vishnu's incarnations in shaping the cultural and religious landscape.

Continuing with Vishnu's incarnations:

In the Vamana-Avatar, Vishnu takes the form of a dwarf Brahmin to subdue the demon king Bali. With each step, Vamana covers the entire universe, reestablishing cosmic order.

The Parashurama-Avatar portrays Vishnu as a warrior with an axe, exterminating oppressive Kshatriya rulers to restore dharma, or righteousness.

In the Rama-Avatar, Vishnu incarnates as Prince Rama, showcasing ideal leadership and devotion. This narrative, found in the epic Ramayana, holds cultural significance.

The Krishna-Avatar, a central figure in the Mahabharata and the Bhagavad Gita, depicts Vishnu as Lord Krishna. Krishna imparts spiritual wisdom and addresses the cosmic balance, symbolized in his divine teachings.

The Buddha-Avatar, less prominent in mainstream Hinduism, is considered by some as an incarnation of Vishnu. This concept emerged during a period of religious transition in ancient India.

Kalki, the future incarnation, is anticipated as a warrior on a white horse, foretold to restore dharma in a time of moral decline.

Vishnu's avatars exemplify diverse roles, emphasizing the dynamic nature of the divine in responding to cosmic challenges and maintaining order in the universe. These stories hold deep cultural and philosophical significance in Hindu traditions.

To complement Brahma's creative force and Vishnu's preservative role, we encounter Shiva, the third member of the Hindu Trimurti. Shiva represents the destructive aspect of the cosmic cycle, leading to regeneration and renewal.

Shiva is often depicted with a third eye, symbolizing spiritual insight, and a crescent moon on his head. His blue throat, known as Neelakantha, results from consuming the poison generated during the churning of the cosmic ocean.

Shiva's consort, Parvati, embodies the divine feminine and is a manifestation of Adi Shakti, the primal energy. Together, they symbolize the complementary forces of creation and destruction.

The various forms of Shiva, such as Nataraja (Lord of Dance), depict him performing the cosmic dance of destruction and creation. The dance signifies the perpetual cycles of birth, life, death, and rebirth.

Shiva's presence extends to Mount Kailash, believed to be his abode, and the sacred river Ganges, which flows from his locks. Devotees revere Shiva in numerous temples and celebrate festivals like Maha Shivaratri in his honor.

Hinduism recognizes other deities, each contributing to the diverse facets of the divine. Goddess Lakshmi, associated with wealth and prosperity, and Saraswati, the embodiment of knowledge and arts, exemplify the richness of Hindu pantheon.

In summary, Hinduism's vibrant tapestry of deities reflects the dynamic interplay of cosmic forces. Brahma's creation, Vishnu's preservation, and Shiva's destruction encapsulate the eternal cycle of existence, guided by principles of dharma and devotion.

In a more contemporary context, Varunani, revered as the goddess of beauty, is known as Lakshmi or Shri. It's interesting to note that, like the Greek Aphrodite, she is said to originate from the ocean's froth.

Vishnu's third incarnation, Varâha-avatar, takes the form of a wild boar to defeat the demon Hiranyaksha, who posed a threat to the world.

The narrative continues with Hiranya-Kasipu's son, Prahlada, a devout Vishnu devotee. Despite his father's attempts to harm him, Prahlada remains unscathed through constant prayer. When Hiranya-Kasipu doubts Vishnu's omnipresence, a furious Vishnu appears as Narasinha-avatar, a half-man, half-lion creature, tearing the skeptic apart. This story aims to emphasize the consequences for those who doubt Vishnu's existence.

The tale proceeds to Balis, Prahlada's grandson, a righteous king nearing completion of a grand sacrifice. To protect the gods, Vishnu assumes the form of a dwarf Brahman mendicant. Balis, in his generosity, agrees to grant the dwarf three paces of land. The dwarf transforms, covering the entire earth, atmosphere, and heavens in three steps, thwarting Balis' plans. This incarnation is known as Vamana-avatar.

The Parashura-avatar, the sixth incarnation, delves into historical context, portraying the struggles between the warrior and Brahman castes for supremacy. The narrative unfolds with Jamadagni, a pious Brahman, and Karttavirya, a warrior-king. Karttavirya's greed leads to conflict, culminating in Râma, Vishnu's incarnation, defeating the oppressive king with divine powers and a battle-ax.

These stories contribute to the diverse tapestry of Hindu mythology, conveying moral lessons and emphasizing the significance of faith and virtue.

The seventh incarnation of Vishnu is known as the Rama Chandra-avatar. This avatar is renowned for the heroic narrative of Rama, assisted by the Monkey King Hanuman, as they vanquish Ravana, a powerful antagonist. The story unfolds with the abduction of Rama's wife, Sita, by Ravana, leading to a epic battle and the eventual triumph of good over evil.

Moving forward, the eighth incarnation, known as the Krishna-avatar, holds a prominent place in Hindu mythology. Vishnu is born as Krishna, miraculously escaping persecution by the tyrant of Mathura. The tales of Krishna include his childhood exploits, his role in the Mahabharata, and the delivery of the Bhagavad Gita, a sacred scripture that forms a significant part of Hindu philosophy.

VISHNU IN THE FORM OF RÂMA CHANDRA. (Fragment of a car. Musée Guimet.)
Click to view
VISHNU IN THE FORM OF RÂMA CHANDRA. (Fragment of a car. Musée Guimet.)

The Krishna-avatar is characterized by divine feats, compassionate teachings, and enduring love. Krishna's divine play, or "Leela," captures the hearts of devotees and emphasizes the divine nature of Vishnu.

As the tales continue, the ninth incarnation is the Buddha-avatar. This avatar reflects a shift in perspective, presenting

Buddha, the historical figure, as an embodiment of Vishnu's compassionate and enlightened nature. The Buddha-avatar signifies the importance of wisdom, compassion, and the pursuit of truth.

The tenth and final incarnation is prophesied to be the Kalki-avatar, a yet-to-occur event where Vishnu will appear as Kalki, the warrior on a white horse, to bring an end to the current age of darkness and corruption. This future avatar symbolizes the ultimate triumph of righteousness and the restoration of cosmic order.

In summary, the avatars of Vishnu in Hindu mythology provide a rich tapestry of narratives, moral teachings, and divine manifestations, each contributing to the multifaceted understanding of the divine in the Hindu tradition.

The Rama Chandra avatar has deeply influenced the Indian psyche and is chronicled in the Ramayana, often regarded as the Hindu equivalent of the Odyssey, sharing similarities with the tale of Rama.

Rama Chandra, accompanied by his wife Sita (sometimes seen as an incarnation of Lakshmi) and his half-brother Lakshmana, resided in the southern wilderness after being unjustly banished by his father. Ravana, the demon-king, waged war against Rama, abducting Sita during a hunting expedition. The epic unfolds with Rama's battles against giants and demons, aided by allies like the monkey kings, Lugriva and Hanuman. Hanuman's courageous journey to Lanka, the construction of a stone bridge by the monkeys over the strait, and Rama's pursuit of Ravana culminate in the defeat of Ravana and the joyous reunion with Sita.

Similar to the sixth avatar, the Rama Chandra avatar likely

contains historical echoes and bears resemblances to Western epics such as the Trojan War and the Gudrun Saga, all centering around the theme of an abducted wife. The mythic essence of these narratives often mirrors the sun god's quest for his consort, the moon.

In the eighth incarnation, Krishna, Vishnu embodies the ideal man-god in Hinduism. The narrative begins with the tyrant Kansa's attempt to thwart a prophecy that predicted his downfall at the hands of his sister Devaki's eighth son. Krishna, an incarnation of Vishnu, miraculously survives Kansa's attempts on his life. Krishna's childhood is marked by various adventures, including the defeat of formidable foes like the serpent king Kali-naga and the giant Shishoo-polu. His youth is characterized by charming the lasses of Gokula with his flute and fostering protection for the cowherds. The tale concludes with Krishna vanquishing Kansa and ascending to the throne.

These avatars, deeply embedded in Hindu mythology, offer profound insights into moral lessons, historical echoes, and the divine manifestations of Vishnu.

In the ninth incarnation, Vishnu takes the form of Buddha, who is considered a divine teacher in Hinduism. The Buddha avatar represents a departure from traditional Vedic rituals and emphasizes compassion, non-violence, and the path to enlightenment. This incarnation is seen as a response to changing times and the need for a shift in spiritual understanding.

The tenth and final avatar of Vishnu is Kalki, a prophesied future incarnation who is expected to appear in a time of great crisis. Kalki is envisioned as a warrior on a white horse, wielding a sword, and is destined to bring an end to corruption and restore righteousness.

Throughout these avatars, Vishnu's manifestations serve various purposes – from restoring cosmic order and defeating evil forces to imparting wisdom and guiding humanity on the path of righteousness. Each avatar reflects the dynamic nature of the divine in response to the challenges and needs of the world.

In summary, the ten avatars of Vishnu provide a rich tapestry of mythology, history, and moral teachings within Hinduism. They showcase the adaptability of the divine to different circumstances and the enduring quest for balance, justice, and spiritual evolution.

In the Mahabharata, often considered the Hindu equivalent of the Iliad, Krishna takes center stage. This epic narrates the war between the Kuru and Pandu clans, both descendants of Bharata and grandchildren of Vyasa. The story revolves around Dhritarashtra, the blind king of the Kurus, and the rivalry between his sons and the Pandus, who initially faced exile due to a rigged game of dice.

Krishna's role becomes crucial when Duryodhana, a Kuru prince, seeks his aid. Although Krishna chooses not to fight directly, he serves as Arjuna's charioteer and imparts profound philosophical teachings, as captured in the Bhagavadgita. The Pandus eventually triumph over the Kurus, and Yudhishthira assumes the throne.

Beyond the war, the Mahabharata delves into various adventures, with the Pandus finding peace and happiness in heaven after their deaths. The narrative portrays the Pandus favorably, contrasting them with the less honorable Kurus.

Krishna, a revered figure akin to Hindu deities like Apollo, Orpheus, and Hercules, plays a multifaceted role. His adventures, reminiscent of mythological and biblical tales, contribute to his esteemed status in the Brahman tradition.

In his ninth avatar, Vishnu takes the form of Buddha, emphasizing moral teachings, purity, charity, and compassionate love. The relationship between the Brahmanic Buddha avatar and Gautama, the historical Buddha, remains complex. Despite historical distinctions, both have influenced each other, with Gautama's teachings shaping the Brahmanic Buddha ideal.

The acceptance of Buddha into the Hindu Pantheon highlights the dynamic interplay between historical figures and idealized deities in Hindu mythology.

Another significant avatar of Vishnu is Krishna, who plays a pivotal role in the Mahabharata, an epic comparable to the Iliad. This narrative centers on the conflict between the Kuru and Pandu clans, descendants of Bharata and grandchildren of Vyasa. The blind Kuru king, Dhritarashtra, allows Bhishma, his uncle, to rule in his stead. The Pandu prince Arjuna, skilled in archery, excels in a test, leading to Yudhishthira's installment as heir.

Despite this, the Kurus attempt to burn the Pandus alive. Surviving in disguise as mendicant Brahmans, the Pandus return, and through strategic alliances, including a marriage to Draupadi, they regain their position. However, a rigged dice game at a festival results in the Pandus losing their kingdom, possessions, and Draupadi. The Kurus promise to return their share of the kingdom after thirteen years, but they renege, leading to a war on the battlefield of Kurukshetra.

Krishna, a revered figure, acts as Arjuna's charioteer during the battle. The Bhagavadgita, a conversation between Krishna and Arjuna, delves into profound philosophical concepts. The Pandus emerge victorious, with Yudhishthira becoming king.

The Mahabharata, while portraying the Pandus favorably, also reflects the flaws of both parties. Krishna, akin to figures like Apollo and Hercules, holds a special place in Hindu mythology. His diverse adventures, including miraculous escapes and battles, contribute to his revered status.

In the ninth avatar, Vishnu incarnates as Buddha, emphasizing moral teachings. The relationship between the Hindu Buddha avatar and Gautama, the historical Buddha, is complex. While they may be distinct, their influence on each other is evident, showcasing the intricate interplay between historical figures and idealized deities in Hindu mythology. The acceptance of Buddha into the Hindu Pantheon demonstrates the adaptability and inclusivity of Hindu religious traditions.

Shifting to another deity, Shiva, often depicted with his consort Parvati, is a central figure in Hinduism. A complex and multifaceted god, Shiva is revered as both a benevolent deity and a formidable force of destruction. In the Trimurti, a concept highlighting the three primary aspects of the divine, Shiva represents the role of the destroyer, balancing the creative and preservative forces embodied by Brahma and Vishnu, respectively.

One of the iconic symbols associated with Shiva is the linga, representing the creative energy of the god. In the Shiva-Trimurti depiction, Shiva leans on the linga, emphasizing his

connection to the generative aspect of existence. The sacred
bull, Nandi, often accompanies Shiva, symbolizing strength
and unwavering loyalty.

Jagannath, a deity particularly revered in the eastern parts
of India, is another manifestation of Vishnu. Often depicted
with two companions, Jagannath is associated with the Rath
Yatra, an annual chariot festival where devotees pull massive
chariots bearing the deities through the streets. This celebration symbolizes the journey of the divine in the world and
attracts millions of pilgrims.

The rich tapestry of Hindu mythology incorporates various deities and avatars, each contributing to the diverse and
dynamic religious landscape. Whether through tales of epic
battles, moral teachings, or cosmic symbolism, Hinduism
reflects a profound exploration of the divine and its multifaceted expressions in the world.

The Hindu pantheon also includes goddesses who play
pivotal roles in the cosmic order. Durga, often depicted riding
a lion and wielding multiple weapons, is a fierce and protective goddess. She is celebrated during the festival of Durga
Puja, symbolizing the triumph of good over evil. Lakshmi,
associated with wealth and prosperity, is another important
goddess, often depicted with lotus flowers and adorned with
jewels.

Saraswati, the goddess of knowledge, arts, and music, is
revered by students and scholars. Her association with the
swan, symbolizing discernment, and the veena, representing
the arts, underscores the importance of wisdom and creativity in human life.

Kali, a manifestation of the goddess Parvati, represents

the destructive aspect of time and the transformative power of creation. Often depicted with a necklace of skulls and a severed head, Kali symbolizes the inevitable cycle of birth, death, and rebirth.

The Hindu pantheon is vast and varied, reflecting the diverse facets of the divine. The deities and their stories serve as a source of inspiration, guidance, and devotion for millions of followers. The rituals, festivals, and practices associated with these deities form an integral part of Hindu religious life, fostering a deep and enduring connection between the divine and the human experience.

In contemporary terms:

The Hindu deity that aligns most closely with the Buddha avatar is Jagannath, the god associated with love and mercy.

The tenth avatar is yet to be realized. It's anticipated that Vishnu will appear on a winged white horse to reward the virtuous, convert sinners, and eradicate all evil.

The horse has one foot raised, and when it sets its foot down, the incarnation will reach its fulfillment.

Siva, the Auspicious One, represents the end of the world and its regeneration in the Indian trinity. Often symbolized by the linga, denoting the creative force, and the all-devouring fire depicted as a flame within a triangle, point upward.

Regarding Siva worship, it's noteworthy that the linga, representing the creative principle, is not associated with indecent ideas or sexual love for Saiva worshippers. The linga transforms from being an object of reverence as a symbol of creation to becoming a wand, staff, and scepter in various contexts.

Siva's consort, Kali, holds a prominent place in Indian

divinity. Known by many names, she embodies the power of nature and the merciless cruelty of natural laws. As Kali, she's identified with time, the all-devourer, and is depicted enjoying destruction, perdition, and murder in various forms.

The pantheistic concept of HariHara, a combination of Vishnu and Siva, symbolizes the unity of these two gods. HariHara is portrayed as a figure that is half male and half female, signifying the harmony between the two deities.

In addition to the major deities, there are numerous secondary gods and goddesses like Ganesa, the elephant-headed god of wisdom, and Kama, the Hindu counterpart of Amor. Additionally, there are various spirits, elves, and demons, each with their own attributes and characteristics in Hindu mythology.

Among these secondary deities, Ganesa stands out with his elephant head, symbolizing wisdom. Kama, often considered the Hindu equivalent of Cupid, is another notable figure associated with love and desire. Karttikeya, riding on a peacock and a son of Siva, is a leader among the good demons.

The Hindu pantheon also includes numerous spirits and supernatural entities. The Gandharvas are considered benevolent sprites, while the Apsaras, akin to Hindu elves, are generally not malevolent. However, a significant number of these entities, such as the Asuras, Pretas (ghosts), Bhutas (spook-spirits), Grahas (baby-killing spirits), and Rakshasas (giants or vampires), are often portrayed as dangerous and demoniacal.

The Mahabharata, a Hindu epic similar to the Wars of the Roses in the West, narrates the tale of the war between the Kurus and Pandus, reflecting both historical struggles and mythical elements. The great hero Arjuna, favored by Krishna, plays a central role in the battle at Kurukshetra. During this conflict, Krishna serves as Arjuna's charioteer and imparts profound philosophical insights, as recorded in the Bhagavadgita.

Looking forward, the tenth avatar of Vishnu, known as Kalki, is anticipated to arrive on a winged white horse. This incarnation is expected to reward the virtuous, convert sinners, and eradicate evil. The symbolism involves the horse lifting its foot, marking the culmination of this incarnation.

Overall, Hindu mythology presents a rich tapestry of deities, spirits, and epic tales that continue to influence cultural and religious practices in contemporary times.

Footnotes

1. Pantheism, derived from the Greek roots πᾶν (pan) meaning "All," and θεός (theos) meaning "God," should not be confused with Pantism, a theory of the All (from πᾶν, root ΠΑΝΤ), which is a distinct concept.

2. Sir Monier-Monier Williams makes a distinction between Brahmanism, the ancient belief of the Indian Aryas, and Hinduism, the modern manifestation of this religion that evolved after the expulsion of Buddhism from India.

3. For the sake of brevity, we refrain from delving into intricate details in this exposition of the ten avatars, omitting certain nuances and variations in the myths.

4. Referring to an English translation from Schwartze's

latest translation by G. R. S. Meade, p. 354, the source material mentions, "MS., P 354."

5. All the avatar illustrations are sourced from Picart.

6. The Pandus, also known as Pandavas, and the Kurus as Kamavas.

7. The shared marriage of Draupadi with the five Pandus suggests the antiquity of the story. While polyandry was not in line with Aryan customs during the Mahabharata's versification era, Vyasa allegorically explains it by equating Draupadi with Lakshmi and the Pandu brothers representing different forms of Indra.

8. Referring to Histoire du Bouddhisme by Eugène Burnouf, I., 338.

9. Legends of the HariHara shrine, translated from the Sanskrit by Rev. Thomas Foulkes.

10. Ganesa, meaning the lord (isa) of hosts (gana), is originally Siva himself. Invoked under this name, Ganesa is called upon by authors to ward off evil demons.

11. Karttikeya, also known as Subrahmanya and Skanda.

8

BUDDHISM

Buddhism emerged as a religious revolution challenging the prevailing flaws within Brahmanism. Gautama Shakyamuni, known as the Buddha or the Enlightened One, rejected practices like bloody sacrifices, blind adherence to the Vedas, reliance on rituals, and the caste system. Instead, he advocated for a moral path attained through enlightenment, or bodhi. Central to his teachings was the idea of eradicating selfishness through an all-encompassing love for all beings as the path to salvation.

The complexity of Buddhism is evident in its diverse interpretations of evil and the quest for liberation from it. Evil is personified as Mara, the Buddhist Devil, embodying temptation, sin, and mortality. Mara's character draws from Indian mythology, where he shares traits with Namuche, a malevolent demon who obstructs rainfall, causing drought.

However, he is ultimately defeated by Indra, the god of thunderstorms, restoring life to the earth.

Mara is also known as Papiyan, the Wicked One, or the Tempter. His alias Varsavarti, meaning "he who fulfils desires," highlights his role as the epitome of selfish desires, representing the insatiable thirst for existence, pleasure, and power. He reigns over the realm of sensual indulgence, symbolizing the allure of self-gratification.

This portrayal of Mara as Varsavarti carries a profound truth: selfishness is likened to Satan, and the fulfillment of selfish desires leads to a metaphorical hell. It echoes the moral lesson found in an anecdote where a man, expecting comfort and indulgence in the afterlife, discovers he's in hell because true happiness lies in aligning oneself with a higher purpose, rather than pursuing personal whims. Similarly, in Buddhist philosophy, the realm of sensual pleasures, ruled by Mara, is equated with hell, emphasizing the folly of self-indulgence.

This understanding sheds light on the core philosophy of Buddhism, emphasizing the importance of transcending selfish desires and ego-driven pursuits. In contrast to the pursuit of personal pleasure and power, Buddhism advocates for a path of selflessness and compassion, guiding individuals towards enlightenment and liberation from suffering.

In essence, the Buddhist conception of Mara serves as a symbolic representation of the human struggle against internal temptations and worldly attachments. By recognizing and overcoming the influence of Mara, practitioners strive to attain a state of inner peace and spiritual freedom.

Moreover, the narrative surrounding Mara offers profound insights into the nature of suffering and the pursuit of genuine happiness. It teaches that true fulfillment cannot be found in the transient pleasures of the material world but lies in transcending the self and cultivating a sense of interconnectedness with all living beings.

Ultimately, the story of Mara underscores the fundamental principles of Buddhist teachings, encouraging individuals to cultivate mindfulness, compassion, and wisdom in their journey towards enlightenment. By understanding the nature of Mara and its implications, practitioners are empowered to navigate the complexities of existence and embark on a path towards profound spiritual awakening.

In the Dhammapada, Mara isn't just a character but more of a symbol, representing temptation and the allure of worldly pleasures. Throughout the text, Mara's name is used allegorically to convey this idea. For instance:

"He who lives solely for pleasure, letting his desires run wild,

Indulging in excess, lazy and weak,

Mara will surely bring him down like a strong wind felling a feeble tree."

Original Buddhism, in its purest form, doesn't dwell on the concept of devils beyond Mara, who symbolizes selfish desires, sensual indulgence, sin, and mortality. However, Buddhist folklore, spanning from ancient Jatakas to modern Chinese and Japanese tales, abounds with various evil spirits, representing life's hardships and the lurking dangers of nature.

While Buddhist teachings depict the consequences of wrongdoing with vivid images of hellish torment akin to

Christian beliefs, they also offer hope in the form of rebirth in the Western Paradise for devout followers.

In the life story of Buddha, Mara assumes a significant role as the obstacle to achieving enlightenment. During Buddha's great renunciation, Mara appears, attempting to dissuade him from his path. Standing in the air, Mara tries to lure Buddha with promises of worldly power and sovereignty, but Buddha remains steadfast, rejecting Mara's deceitful temptations.

In Buddhist teachings, Mara serves as more of a symbol than a literal figure, representing the forces of temptation and distraction that hinder spiritual progress. Throughout Buddhist texts like the Dhammapada, Mara is mentioned allegorically to illustrate the dangers of being consumed by worldly desires and pleasures. For instance:

"The one who lives solely for pleasure, Indulging unchecked in sensory delights, Lazy and unfocused in mind and action, Will surely fall victim to Mara's sway, Like a feeble tree succumbing to a strong wind's force."

Traditional Buddhism, in its purest form, doesn't dwell extensively on the concept of demons beyond Mara. However, Buddhist folklore, ranging from ancient Jatakas to modern tales in regions like China and Japan, often depicts various malevolent spirits representing the trials and tribulations of life.

While Buddhist teachings do describe the consequences of negative actions with vivid depictions of hellish suffering, they also offer the promise of spiritual liberation and rebirth in realms of enlightenment for devout followers.

In the life story of Buddha, Mara assumes a crucial role as the embodiment of obstacles on the path to enlightenment.

During pivotal moments like Buddha's renunciation, Mara appears, attempting to sway him from his spiritual journey with promises of worldly power and wealth. However, Buddha remains steadfast, rejecting Mara's illusions and staying committed to his quest for ultimate truth and liberation.

When Buddha, in his quest for enlightenment, spent seven years immersed in ascetic practices and self-denial, his health deteriorated, leaving him frail and emaciated. It was then that Mara, symbolizing worldly desires and distractions, approached him, suggesting that he abandon his pursuit of enlightenment. According to the Padhana Sutta:

"Mara, speaking with false compassion, said: 'You appear weak and sickly, death is near. It's better to live, O Venerable One! In life, you can still perform good deeds. The path of effort is difficult, hard to tread.'

To Mara's persuasion, Buddha responded firmly: 'O deceiver, why have you come? Even the slightest good deed is irrelevant to me. I possess faith, strength, and understanding. As my body weakens, my mind grows calmer, and my focus sharpens. Living thus, I'm free from craving for sensual pleasures. Witness my inner purity!

"Lust, discontent, hunger, desire, sloth, cowardice, doubt, hypocrisy, and worldly pursuits—these are your forces, Mara. Only the courageous conquer them and find joy. Death in battle is preferable to a defeated life.

"As I see your army and you on your elephant, I prepare to battle so you can't sway me. With understanding, I'll crush your forces like breaking an earthen pot.

"Once my thoughts are under control, I'll travel, teaching

disciples to follow a disciplined life free from desire, leading them to a realm without sorrow.'

And Mara acknowledged defeat, admitting: 'For seven years, I followed the Bhagavat, but found no fault in the Perfectly Enlightened and Thoughtful One.'"

At the Bodhi tree, Mara attempted to shake Buddha's resolve, using his daughters' allurements and even force. Despite Mara's efforts to summon an army, natural disasters, and darkness, Buddha remained unmoved, his resolve unwavering. Eventually, Mara and his followers fled as Buddha's enlightenment prevailed.

After attaining enlightenment, Mara returned, urging Buddha to pass away, but Buddha remained steadfast, undeterred by Mara's temptations.

In Buddha's pursuit of enlightenment, after seven years of rigorous ascetic practices, he found himself weakened and frail. At this critical juncture, Mara, symbolizing worldly desires and distractions, approached him, suggesting that he abandon his quest. In the Padhana Sutta, Mara falsely expressed compassion, remarking on Buddha's physical decline and advocating for a return to worldly life. However, Buddha firmly rejected Mara's persuasion, asserting his commitment to his spiritual path and his inner strength to resist temptation.

Mara, embodying lust, discontent, and other worldly desires, represented an obstacle to Buddha's enlightenment. Despite Mara's attempts to sway him, Buddha remained resolute, recognizing the transient nature of worldly pleasures and the importance of inner purity. He metaphorically confronted Mara's forces, symbolizing the inner struggles of the human condition, and asserted his determination to overcome them through inner discipline and understanding.

Even as Mara summoned natural disasters and darkness in a final attempt to disrupt Buddha's enlightenment, Buddha remained steadfast. With unwavering resolve, he faced Mara's challenges and emerged victorious, attaining enlightenment despite the adversary's efforts.

Following his enlightenment, Mara returned once more, tempting Buddha to abandon his earthly existence. However, Buddha remained steadfast in his commitment to his spiritual journey, undeterred by Mara's allurements. Through his unwavering determination and inner strength, Buddha triumphed over Mara's temptations, embodying the principles of enlightenment and spiritual liberation.

Buddha responded firmly to Mara's provocations:

"I will not pass away, Evil One, until both the ordained members of our order and the lay followers, regardless of gender, have become true practitioners of the teachings. They must be wise, well-trained, proficient in scriptures, diligent in their duties—both major and minor—upright in conduct, adhering to ethical precepts. They must themselves understand the doctrine fully, capable of teaching it, spreading its message, establishing it firmly, elucidating its intricacies, and making it accessible to all. They should be equipped to counter and refute false doctrines with truth whenever they arise, thereby spreading the enlightening truth far and wide.

"I will not depart until my pure teachings have flourished, gained popularity, and become widespread. They must be proclaimed effectively among humanity."

As Buddha's earthly journey neared its end, Mara once

again attempted to sway him, saying, "Pass away now, Lord, from existence." Buddha calmly replied, "Prepare yourself; my ultimate departure is imminent."

In Buddhist art, the figure often depicted holding a double club or vajra—a thunderbolt—is interpreted in various ways. Initially thought to represent Devadatta, a disciple who opposed Buddha's teachings, the interpretation has evolved. It may symbolize excess and indulgence, akin to the Greek figure Silenus, rather than a disciple's opposition.

Mara, often portrayed with the wheel of life—the eternal cycle of birth, death, and rebirth—in his grasp, represents worldly temptations and the transient nature of existence. The wheel symbolizes samsara, the continuous cycle of life, death, and rebirth, depicted in various Buddhist scriptures and artworks. The concept of Mara as the ruler of the world, holding the wheel of life, is evident across different Buddhist traditions, emphasizing the universality of the teachings on impermanence and liberation from worldly desires.

In Buddhist scripture, Mara is depicted as a symbolic figure rather than a literal entity. He represents the temptations and challenges that humans face on their spiritual journey. For example, in the Padhana Sutta, Mara is portrayed as discouraging Buddha from his pursuit of enlightenment by tempting him with the allure of worldly pleasures. However, Buddha remains steadfast in his commitment to his path, rejecting Mara's enticements.

The concept of Mara extends beyond individual temptations to encompass the broader challenges of existence, such as ignorance, desire, and attachment. These are represented in the twelve nidanas, or links of dependent origination, which outline the cycle of suffering and rebirth. Mara symbolizes the force that keeps beings trapped in this cycle, perpetuating suffering through ignorance and craving.

Buddhist art often depicts Mara in various forms, illustrating his role as the adversary of enlightenment. Scenes of Buddha resisting Mara's temptations under the bodhi tree are a common motif, symbolizing the struggle against worldly desires on the path to awakening. Additionally, imagery of Mara holding the wheel of life underscores the transient nature of existence and the impermanence of worldly pleasures.

Overall, Mara serves as a powerful metaphor for the obstacles that humans must overcome to achieve spiritual liberation. By recognizing and confronting Mara's influence, practitioners can cultivate mindfulness, wisdom, and compassion, ultimately transcending the cycle of suffering and attaining liberation.

The Hindu depiction divides existence into six realms: gods, humans, nagas (or snakes), paradise, ghosts, and hell. A similar division is seen in Tibetan art, though less distinctly separated, while Japanese art often shows only five divisions. To highlight the Buddha's pervasive influence sustaining life, Japanese art places a statue of Buddha at the center of the wheel, while Hindu art features a Buddha figure in each division. This central Buddha represents the transformative aspect of life towards enlightenment.

The twelve nidanas, essential in the Buddhist wheel of life, are often represented by twelve small pictures either on or around the wheel. In Japanese depictions, these are clearer, beginning at the bottom, rising to the left, and descending on the right.

The first nidana, ignorance, is depicted as a passionate and brutish figure. The second, constitutions of life or primary forms of organization, is shown as a potter's wheel crafting vessels. This should not be confused with samsara, the eternal round of transmigration.

Awareness, the third nidana, is depicted as a monkey, symbolizing animal sense-perception. The fourth, name and form, representing personality, is shown as a pilot steering a boat.

The fifth nidana, the six fields representing the senses and mind, is portrayed as a human organism. The sixth, contact of the six fields with their objects, is depicted as a lover's embrace.

Sensation or sentiment, the seventh nidana, is illustrated by sighing lovers. From sentiment arises desire or thirst, the eighth nidana, shown as separated lovers flirting.

Clinging to existence, the ninth nidana, is depicted as a lover following their beloved. Existence, the tenth nidana, is illustrated as the union of lovers celebrating their marriage feast.

Birth, the eleventh nidana, is represented by a woman in labor. The twelfth nidana, with its various sufferings, includes old age, disease, death, lamentation, complaints, punishments, and tribulations.

The Hindu wheel presents these nidanas less distinctly but with the same meaning. It starts at the top right with ignorance and progresses through the other nidanas clockwise.

The concept of the wheel of life likely predates Buddhism and might have roots in ancient demonolatry. Similar representations of the world held by a monstrous figure are found in ancient Chaldean artifacts. Over time, religious symbols and rituals persist, even as fundamental beliefs evolve.

In Tibetan Buddhism, demonology is prominent, influenced by Hinduism. Key figures include mKha'sGroma, similar to the Hindu Goddess Kali, depicted as a fearsome monster surrounded by flames.

In China, Taoism, Confucianism, and Buddhism coexist, with reverence paid to Lao-Tsze, Confucius, and Buddha. Japan also features Shintoism alongside Buddhism, with Shintoism recently declared the official state religion.

Chinese Taoism and Japanese Shintoism folklore influenced Buddhist mythology, leading to depictions of hell with figures like Emma, the stern judge, and Kongo, the sheriff. These representations include bailiffs, torturers, and executioners, illustrating concepts of karmic retribution.

Despite the seriousness of hell and its torments, humor is found in Chinese and Japanese devil depictions, like the Oni-no-Nembutzu, the Devil as a monk.

In Northern Buddhism's later development, the evils of the world, represented by various devil figures, are seen as incarnations of Buddha. These devils serve as teachers and instruments of education, contributing to humanity's ultimate salvation through enlightenment.

Christian salvation involves atonement through the sacrifice of a sinless redeemer, while Buddhist salvation is attained through enlightenment, with Buddha serving as a teacher guiding people towards salvation through example and instruction.

The Buddhism of Tibet remains somewhat unexplored due to the country's inaccessibility, but it shows a highly developed demonology with strong Hindu influences. One prominent figure is mKha'sGroma, akin to the fearsome Hindu deity Kali, depicted as a monstrous being with a lion-like head wreathed in flames, ready to consume all in its path.

In China, Taoism, Confucianism, and Buddhism peacefully coexist, with each receiving customary homage in homes throughout the country. Art often depicts Lao-Tsze, Confucius, and Buddha together as guiding influences on China's moral life.

Similarly, in Japan, Buddhism coexists with Shintoism, the indigenous nature-worship of the land. Shintoism, now recognized as the official state religion, involves the observation of national festivals and rituals.

The folklore of Chinese Taoism and Japanese Shintoism has been incorporated into Buddhist mythology, resulting in temple depictions of hell and its denizens. Figures like Emma, the stern judge, and Kongo, the sheriff, are common, along with a host of bailiffs, torturers, and executioners. These representations serve to illustrate concepts of karmic justice and the consequences of one's actions.

While hell and its torments are depicted seriously, there's also room for humor in Chinese and Japanese devil imagery. One such example is the Oni-no-Nembutzu, portraying the Devil in the guise of a monk, a figure that reflects the playful and irreverent side of religious art.

In the later evolution of Northern Buddhism, the various evils of the world, embodied in devilish beings, are viewed as manifestations of Buddha himself. These devils, far from being adversaries of Buddha, are considered his ministers and collaborators in the grand design of educating humanity about the consequences of sin. This interpretation transforms Buddhist devils from mere tormentors into essential components of the path to enlightenment.

In contrast to Christian salvation, which involves atonement through the sacrifice of a sinless redeemer, Buddhist salvation is attained through enlightenment. Buddha serves not as a redeemer but as a teacher, guiding individuals along the path to enlightenment through example and instruction.

The imagery of hell and salvation in Buddhism is rich with symbolism and metaphor, often depicted in vivid detail in temple artwork and religious texts. One such illustration shows Buddha extending help to a suffering soul in hell, emphasizing the idea that even in the depths of suffering, there is the potential for redemption and liberation.

Throughout Buddhist tradition, the concept of karma plays a central role in shaping one's destiny. Karma, the law of cause and effect, dictates that one's actions in this life will have consequences in the next, whether positive or negative. This belief underscores the importance of ethical conduct and mindfulness in Buddhist practice.

In addition to salvation through enlightenment, Buddhism also offers the concept of rebirth or reincarnation. According to Buddhist teachings, individuals undergo a cycle of death and rebirth, with the quality of each new life determined by the accumulated karma from past actions. This cycle continues until one achieves enlightenment and breaks free from the cycle of samsara, or the cycle of birth and death.

In summary, the Buddhist worldview encompasses a rich tapestry of beliefs and practices aimed at alleviating suffering and attaining spiritual liberation. From intricate depictions of hell and salvation to the fundamental principles of karma and rebirth, Buddhism offers a comprehensive framework for understanding the nature of existence and the path to awakening.

Footnotes

1. Papiyan, derived from the Sanskrit "papin," means "very wicked" or "more wicked."

2. "Varsavarti" in Sanskrit, or "Vasavatti" in Pali, originates from "vasa," meaning wish or desire. Mara is also known as "Paranimmita Vasavatti," signifying control over what others create.

3. "Tanha" in Pali or "trishna" in Sanskrit.

4. Refer to Sacred Books of the East, Vol. X, second part, pages 69-71.

5. See "Buddhistische Kunst in Indien" by L. A. Waddell, M. B., M. R. A. S., p. 87.

6. The Visudhi Magga states that karma-existence is tantamount to existence.

7. The term "confection" poorly translates to "formation" or "deed-form." Refer to The Dharma, pages 16-18.

8. Described by L. A. Waddell, M. B., M. R. A. S., in the Journal of the Royal Asiatic Society, April 1894. Also, see the lavish color reproduction on Plate 8, Vol. I., of "The Paintings in the Buddhist Cave Temples of Ajanta" by John Griffiths. London, Griggs, 1896.

9. The Tibetan and Japanese illustrations are elucidated by Professor Bastian in his "Ethnologisches Bilderbuch."

10. It's worth noting that in certain regions of India, the

serpent symbolizes wisdom and perfection. This belief was adopted by the Ophites, a Gnostic sect that revered the serpent from the Garden of Eden as the teacher of knowledge and the originator of science.

9

THE DAWN OF A NEW ERA

Gnostic Societies and Congregations

As the Old Testament gave way to the New, an era of upheaval unfolded. Jewish society had been influenced by Assyrian, Babylonian, and Persian cultures, and the exchange of ideas across Western Asia intensified after Alexander the Great. Greek and Indian philosophies mingled, sparking a transformative shift in religious beliefs. Hindu doctrines, albeit in vague and sometimes contradictory forms, reached Syria, challenging traditional ethics. While procreation and wealth acquisition had been revered, the allure of salvation through chastity and poverty emerged.

Three key concepts drove this movement: the spirituality of the soul, the yearning for liberation from physical existence, and the pursuit of enlightenment or wisdom.

The pinnacle of Gnostic aspiration, termed "fulfilment" or πλήρωμα, was envisioned either as individual salvation akin to Buddhist Nirvana or as universal redemption through a messianic figure.

This spirit of inquiry led to the formation of religious communities, akin to modern theosophical movements. Urban centers hosted groups of students delving into salvation and immortality, alongside practitioners applying these principles in daily life. The former were known as "learners" or disciples (μαθηταί), while the latter were termed "holy ones" or healers (ἅγιοι or θεραπευταί).

Among the diverse sects, the Gnostics of Syria stood out. Dubbed "serpent-worshippers" or Ophites by Church leaders, they viewed Yahveh, the creator of the material world, as malevolent upon encountering the Bible. Conversely, they revered the serpent, symbolizing enlightenment, as a messenger of the true, benevolent God. This deity, they proclaimed, was triune: the Father, representing the human prototype; the Son, embodying eternal reason; and the Spirit, symbolizing spiritual generation.

Similar concepts regarding the triune Godhead and deliverance from evil are attributed to various sects, notably Simon Magus, mentioned in Acts as having been baptized by St. Peter but condemned for believing the Holy Ghost could be purchased.

In Judæa, amidst sects like the Nazarenes, Sabians (or Baptisers), Essenes, and Ebionites, emerged a distinct third party from the orthodox Pharisees and liberal Sadducees, primarily comprising the poorer class. Notably, Jesus of

Nazareth emerged from this milieu to champion a new faith and embody a new religion.

The Apocrypha of the Old Testament

During this era, literature not included in the Old Testament canon, known as the Apocrypha, emerged. Despite its merit, it's deemed apocryphal due to exclusion from the canon.

A new worldview emphasizing the dichotomy between body and soul brought forth a fresh moral ideal. In these apocryphal texts, Satan evolved into a mythological, dualistic entity—an independent evil demon, potentially influenced by Persian beliefs, opposing both man and God.

For instance, in the story of Tobit, an evil spirit named Asmodi, likely of Persian origin, obstructs Sarah's marriage due to his own affection for her. In the Talmud, Asmodi morphs into a demon of lust.

Among the Apocrypha, books like Daniel and Esdras hold value, though sometimes marred by Judaistic bias and animosity toward Gentile nations. Esdras, particularly, anticipates Christian eschatology, even mentioning a Saviour named Jesus.

Esdras introduces two abyssal beings, Enoch and Leviathan, though they play no role in evil's origin. God, through an angel, explains the genesis of evil using a parable akin to the Buddhist story of Nirvana and Christ's Sermon on the Mount, illustrating the narrow path to salvation amidst perilous obstacles.

This unique apocryphal work is attributed to the patriarch

Enoch. Enoch's story, preserved in various ancient texts, offers insights into ancient Jewish cosmology, angelology, and eschatology. The text known as 1 Enoch, composed in several parts over time, includes vivid descriptions of heavenly visions, the fallen angels known as Watchers, and the coming judgment. It was highly regarded by some early Jewish and Christian communities, influencing beliefs about the end times and the nature of evil.

Enoch's journey through the heavens and encounters with celestial beings provide a fascinating glimpse into ancient Jewish mysticism and religious thought. His apocalyptic visions, filled with symbolic imagery and cosmic battles, captivated the imagination of later generations and contributed to the rich tapestry of Jewish and Christian literature.

Despite its exclusion from the biblical canon, the Book of Enoch remains a significant and influential work in the history of religious literature, offering valuable insights into the beliefs and concerns of ancient Jewish and early Christian communities. Its themes of divine judgment, angelic rebellion, and the fate of the righteous continue to resonate with readers today, sparking curiosity and inspiring further exploration into the mysteries of the spiritual realm.

The Book of Enoch delves into an allegorical exploration of God's design for the world's history. While not explicitly Christian, it bears resemblance to doctrines upheld by sects that emerged around the dawn of Christianity, vying for followers alongside it.

Enoch's discussion of demons reflects the religious myths prevalent among the Gentiles, while his concepts of salvation from evil hint at Gnostic inclinations.

For instance, Chapter 42 depicts Wisdom's futile search for a home among humanity before returning to her celestial abode among the angels.

Regarding the Messiah, often referred to as "the son of a woman," or "the son of man," and occasionally as "the son of God," the text suggests his preexistence:

"Before the sun and the signs of the zodiac, before the stars of the heavens were created, his name was spoken before the Lord of the spirits. Chosen and concealed before the creation of the world, he remains hidden before Him [God], existing from eternity to eternity."

"All the secrets of wisdom will flow from his mouth, for the Lord of the spirits has granted him wisdom and glorified him. The spirit of wisdom dwells within him, along with the spirit of understanding, doctrine, power, and the spirits of all the justified, even those who sleep. He will judge all hidden matters, and none will dare speak trivialities before him, for he is chosen by the Lord of the spirits. He is powerful in matters of justification, and injustice cannot stand before him."

God expresses his intent to join with the sons of the earth eternally, walking in righteousness throughout their lives.

The spiritual insights presented in the Book of Enoch, particularly the portrayal of the Messiah as a supernatural figure, align more with Essene or Gnostic beliefs than with Christian doctrine, which emphasizes the Messiah's incarnation as a flesh-and-blood human.

Unfortunately, we only have an Ethiopian translation of the Book of Enoch, rendered into German by Dr. A. Dillmann. Nonetheless, it remains a valuable resource for historians, reflecting a Judaistic strain of Gnosticism. It is speculated that the original Book of Enoch was penned around 110 B.C. by a Pharisaic Jewish author.

The Book of Enoch offers an allegorical journey through God's overarching plan for the history of the world. Although not explicitly aligned with Christianity, it mirrors doctrines embraced by various sects that emerged around the onset of Christianity, seeking adherents alongside it.

Enoch's exploration of demons reflects the mythological narratives prevalent among the Gentiles, while his discussions on salvation from evil suggest inclinations toward Gnostic thought.

In Chapter 42, we encounter Wisdom's quest for a place among humanity, only to return to her celestial abode among the angels, symbolizing the elusive nature of divine wisdom.

Regarding the Messiah, referred to as "the son of a woman," "the son of man," and occasionally "the son of God," the text hints at his preexistence:

"Before the sun, the zodiac signs, and the stars were created, his name resounded before the Lord of the spirits. Chosen and concealed before the world's inception, he remains hidden before God, existing from eternity to eternity."

The passage continues, highlighting the Messiah's role as the bearer of divine wisdom and the judge of all concealed matters, endowed with the spirit of understanding, doctrine, power, and righteousness.

God's intention to unite with the sons of the earth, walking alongside them in righteousness throughout their lives, underscores the divine desire for communion with humanity.

The spiritual insights presented in the Book of Enoch, particularly regarding the supernatural nature of the Messiah, align more closely with Essene or Gnostic beliefs than with mainstream Christian doctrine, which emphasizes the Messiah's incarnation as a human being.

Although only an Ethiopian translation of the Book of Enoch exists, translated into German by Dr. A. Dillmann, it remains a valuable resource for historians, shedding light on Judaistic Gnostic tendencies. Scholars speculate that the original Book of Enoch was penned around 110 B.C. by a Jewish author associated with the Pharisaic tradition.

The Book of Wisdom, originating from Alexandrian Judaism and influenced by Greek and Eastern thought, attributes the introduction of death into the world to the Devil's envy. It states:

"God created man to be immortal, reflecting his own eternal nature. However, death entered the world through the Devil's envy, and those who follow his path find themselves subject to it."

The Wisdom literature bears marks of Indian influence, with the term "wisdom" (sophia) possibly echoing the Sanskrit "bodhi." Additionally, the concept of a trinity begins to emerge in Jewish thought, initially modeled after the familial structure of father, mother, and child. In these writings, Sophia is depicted as God's spouse, with the Messiah portrayed as their offspring. Some Gnostic groups later utilized terms like Sophia, Pneuma, and Logos to describe the second aspect of the divine, highlighting the maternal aspect of the God-man. However, within early Christian development, the concept of a divine mother figure was abandoned, and the Logos was identified as God the Son, the second person of the Trinity, while the term Pneuma or Spirit remained for the third person.

This notion of a Trinity, although absent from the New Testament and deemed spurious in certain passages, became a prominent feature in Gnostic systems, often appearing as abstract principles or familial relationships within the divine. Notably, in the Gospel according to the Hebrews, Christ refers to the Holy Ghost as his mother.

The Trinity concept has ancient roots, seen in Babylonian, Brahmanic, and Buddhist traditions. Buddhists, for instance, venerate the Buddha, the Dharma (the teachings), and the Sangha (the community of practitioners) as the "three jewels." While the Trinity doctrine isn't explicitly stated in the New Testament, it plays a significant role in most Gnostic frameworks, depicting a divine unity of Father, Mother, and Child.

Oriental Christians retained this triadic view of God until the rise of Islam. In the Quran, the Christian Trinity is presented as consisting of God, Christ, and Mary, reflecting Gnostic influences. This Gnostic Trinity concept influenced Roman Catholic devotion to Mary, sometimes even integrating her into the Trinity.

Jacob Böhme, a German mystic born in the late 16th century, epitomizes a revival of Gnostic thought. His philosophy, emerging from a deep reflection on the Bible, depicts God as the unfathomable ground of existence, termed the Ungrund. Böhme's monistic view sees evil as a necessary aspect rooted in the divine nature itself. He views the correlation of forces through triads, reflecting divine manifestation and the interplay of good and evil.

Böhme's philosophy challenges readers to seek spiritual illumination beyond literal interpretations of scripture, emphasizing the importance of the Holy Spirit as the key to understanding divine essence. While not a dualist, Böhme envisions a trinity of principles—eternal goodness, eternal badness, and their eternal mixture—represented in every aspect of existence.

The Gnostic movement, including its Jewish phase, played a significant role in paving the way for Christianity by introducing innovative religious ideals. Many Christian doctrines find tentative expression in Old Testament Apocrypha, laying the groundwork for the emergence of Christianity as an organized institution under the leadership of Jesus of Nazareth.

The Gnostic movement and its Jewish phase were instrumental in laying the groundwork for Christianity by introducing novel religious concepts. Within the Old Testament Apocrypha, we see early expressions of many Christian doctrines, such as the bodily resurrection of the dead and the coming of the Messiah, albeit in a tentative form.

The emergence of Christianity as an organized institution was greatly influenced by the Gnostic ferment of the time. Jesus of Nazareth, with his powerful personality and teachings, became a focal point around which these innovative ideas crystallized into a cohesive belief system. Christianity, thus, emerged as a significant force in shaping the course of history.

Jacob Böhme's philosophy, which reflected Gnostic tendencies, offered a unique perspective on the nature of existence and the problem of evil. Rooted in deep reflection on the Bible, Böhme's monistic view saw evil as an intrinsic aspect of the divine, necessitating a deeper understanding of spiritual truths beyond literal interpretations of scripture.

Overall, the Gnostic movement, with its emphasis on spiritual illumination and the interplay of divine forces, contributed to the rich tapestry of religious thought, influencing both ancient and modern understandings of theology and philosophy.

The Book of Wisdom, originating from Alexandrian Judaism and influenced by Greek and Eastern philosophies, discusses the introduction of death into the world by the Devil out of envy. This work reflects a fusion of diverse cultural influences, suggesting a broader understanding of religious concepts.

Within the Wisdom literature, we find echoes of Indian influence, particularly in the use of the term "wisdom" (sophia), reminiscent of the Sanskrit term "bodhi." Additionally, the concept of a trinity begins to emerge, initially modeled after familial relationships, with Wisdom depicted as the spouse of God and the Messiah as their son.

Although not distinctly Christian, this trinity idea laid the groundwork for later Christian interpretations. While some Gnostic groups used terms like Sophia, Pneuma, and Logos to represent divine principles, early Christian thinkers eventually identified the Logos as God the Son, solidifying the concept of the Trinity as Father, Son, and Holy Spirit.

This notion of a divine trinity finds parallels in other religious traditions, such as Babylonian, Brahmanic, and Buddhist beliefs. In Buddhism, for instance, the Three Jewels symbolize the Buddha, the Dharma (teachings), and the Sangha (community), reflecting a similar triadic structure.

Jacob Böhme, a German mystic influenced by Gnostic ideas, developed a unique philosophical system that mirrored Gnostic thought in many ways. Despite his limited education, Böhme's reflections on the Bible led him to conceive of God as the unfathomable source of existence, embodying both light and darkness, good and evil, in a unified whole.

Böhme's philosophy delves into the problem of evil, positing that it arises from the necessary manifestation of divine will and exists as an inherent aspect of God's nature. His monistic view sees all of existence as interconnected, with goodness and evil intertwined in a complex unity.

In conclusion, the Gnostic movement, with its diverse philosophical currents and mystical insights, played a significant role in shaping the development of Christianity and broader religious thought. Through works like the Book of Wisdom and the writings of figures like Jacob Böhme, we see the enduring influence of Gnostic ideas on theological discourse and spiritual inquiry.

Footnotes:

1. Philo suggests that "therapeutae" may also mean "worshippers." Some scholars, like E. Lucius, have questioned the authenticity of Philo's work "De vita contemplativa" and therefore the existence of the therapeutae. However, these doubts have been convincingly countered by Fred. C. Conybeare in "Philo About the Contemplative Life" (Clarendon Press, Oxford, 1895).

2. The term "Sabian" is derived from the word "tsabha," meaning "to baptize." St. John the Baptist was associated with the Sabians.

3. The word "Essenes" may have multiple origins, including from the Hebrew root "chasah," meaning "to fly" or "to take refuge." Philo suggests they may be called "Essenes" due to their holiness or piety. The term "Ebionites" means "the poor." Early Christians were closely linked with the Nazarenes, with St. Paul being accused of leading the sect of the Nazarenes by Jewish authorities in 54 CE.

4. The name "Nazarene" is distinct from "Nazarite," which refers to someone who abstains from certain practices. Both terms may stem from the root "nazar," meaning "to separate."

5. The authenticity of certain passages, such as the one mentioned, may be questioned as possible later interpolations.

6. For further reading on the Book of Enoch, see Dillmann's "Das Buch Henoch."

7. Jerome, in his work "Adversus Pelagianos," mentions this passage.

8. Jacob Böhme's works include "Hohe und teife Gründe von dem Dreyfachen Leben des Menschen nach dem Geheimnüss der drey Principien göttlicher Offenbahrung" (Amsterdam, 1682) and "Beschreibung der drey Principien göttlichen Wesens" (Amsterdam, 1682).

10

EARLY CHRISTIANITY

Jesus and the New Testament:

During the time of Christ, the concept of evil, particularly embodied by Satan, held significant sway over people's imaginations. References to Satan are frequent in the synoptic gospels, the writings of the Apostles, especially St. Paul, and in the Book of Revelation. While Jesus acknowledged the belief in demonic possession as a cause of mental illness, he spoke less about the Devil compared to his contemporaries.

In the Gospels, Jesus faces temptation from the Devil, mirroring Buddha's encounter with Mâra, the Evil One. Both stories share notable similarities in their details.

Jesus vividly describes the dire consequences of sin, likening the last judgment to fishermen separating good fish from bad. Hell is portrayed as eternal fire and torment, where the wicked face everlasting punishment. The Devil is depicted as the adversary who sows discord, even rebuking one of his close disciples, Peter, as Satan when he speaks contrary to divine will.

While Jesus drew from traditional notions of Satan as a symbol of evil, his primary focus was on moral wickedness rather than a literal embodiment of evil.

The Gospel narratives suggest that Jesus believed in a justice where the present order would be reversed in the future. The story of Dives and Lazarus illustrates this inversion, where earthly disparities are rectified in the afterlife.

The Apostle Paul, echoing Christ's teachings, believed in the imminent return of Christ. He encouraged believers not to be shaken by worldly concerns, as he himself anticipated witnessing the day of the Lord. This expectation of Christ's imminent return shaped the early Christian mindset, emphasizing spiritual readiness for the coming kingdom.

Paul's confidence in the imminent return of Christ influenced his teachings and comforted believers, particularly when facing death. He assured the Thessalonian Christians that those who had died would be resurrected and united with the living at Christ's return. Paul was so certain of this event that he considered his words as divine revelation.

In essence, the New Testament presents Jesus as acknowledging the reality of evil, symbolized by Satan, but focusing more on the moral consequences of sin rather than engaging in detailed discussions about the Devil. His teachings emphasize the importance of spiritual readiness for the coming kingdom of God and the assurance of justice in the afterlife, where earthly injustices will be rectified. This belief in the imminent return of Christ deeply influenced early Christian thought, shaping their outlook on life and death.

"If we believe that Jesus died and rose again, then we also believe that God will bring with Jesus those who have fallen asleep in him. For this we declare to you by the word of the Lord, that we who are alive, who are left until the coming of the Lord, will by no means precede those who have died. For the Lord himself, with a cry of command, with the archangel's call and with the sound of God's trumpet, will descend from heaven, and the dead in Christ will rise first. Then we who are alive, who are left, will be caught up in the clouds together with them to meet the Lord in the air; and so we will be with the Lord forever. Therefore encourage one another with these words."

When early followers of Jesus grew discouraged over his delayed return, a prominent leader wrote a letter to strengthen their faith, especially in the face of ridicule from non-believers. In the second epistle of St. Peter, it's written:

"Dear friends, this is now my second letter to you. I have written both of them as reminders to stimulate you to wholesome thinking. I want you to recall the words spoken in the past by the holy prophets and the command given by our Lord and Savior through your apostles. Above all, you must understand that in the last days scoffers will come, scoffing and following their own evil desires. They will say, 'Where is this 'coming' he promised? Ever since our ancestors died, everything goes on as it has since the beginning of creation.' ... But do not forget this one thing, dear friends: With the Lord a day is like a thousand years, and a thousand years are like a day. The Lord is not slow in keeping his promise, as some understand slowness. Instead he is patient with you, not wanting anyone to perish, but everyone to come to repentance. But the day of the Lord will come like a thief. The heavens will disappear with a roar; the elements will be destroyed by fire, and the earth and everything done in it will be laid bare. ... So then, dear friends, since you are looking forward to this, make every effort to be found spotless, blameless and at peace with him."

The present world remains under the influence of evil until the prophecy of Jesus' return is fulfilled, so it's important to be prepared for spiritual battles. As written in the first epistle of St. Peter:

"Be alert and of sober mind. Your enemy the devil prowls around like a roaring lion looking for someone to devour."

Besides the traditional names like Satan, Beelzebub, and Devil, the New Testament refers to evil as the prince of this world, the great dragon, the old serpent, the prince of the devils, and the Antichrist. Satan is depicted as the founder of an empire that opposes the kingdom of God on earth. Though powerful, Satan is ultimately defeated by Christ, but remains a threat.

A newly discovered book of Daniel contains a story that reflects the early Church's expectations. It tells of a man in Syria, a Christian leader, who persuaded many believers to go into the wilderness to meet Christ. This belief in the imminent return of Christ was prevalent but declined over time, only to resurge around the year 1000, leading to chaos and suffering as people anticipated the end times.

This belief in the imminent return of Christ was prevalent but declined over time, only to resurge around the year 1000, leading to chaos and suffering as people anticipated the end times. Many squandered their wealth to enjoy their final days, while others sold all they had and gave to the poor. Some invested their possessions in church donations and masses. However, this fervor often resulted in widespread poverty and distress among those who believed the end was near.

Over the centuries, the understanding of Christ's return has evolved, with many Christians now interpreting it symbolically or as an event whose timing remains unknown. Yet the hope for a future fulfillment of Christ's promise remains a central tenet of Christian faith, offering comfort and encouragement to believers in every age.

Jewish-Christian Eschatology:

The Revelation of St. John, penned between 68 and 70 A.D., falls into the realm of early Christian beliefs about the end times. It draws heavily from Jewish traditions found in the prophetic books of the Old Testament Apocrypha.

The author, likely a Jew-Christian, addresses the seven churches of Asia Minor, condemning the Nicolaitanes, a Gnostic sect, for their antinomian views. These Nicolaitanes, as per Irenaeus, didn't see adherence to Mosaic law as necessary for salvation. There's a subtle jab at figures like St. Paul, who shared similar antinomian principles, even dining with pagans without concern for dietary laws.

In an uncomfortable passage in chapter 2, verses 20-29, a follower of Pauline Christianity in Thyatira is called out. This might refer to Lydia, a seller of purple, baptized by Paul. The promises of reward from the Lord, as conveyed through

John the Divine, are reserved for those who adhere to the law, hinting at a bias towards Jewish Christians.

The imagery of Christ's triumphant rule over the nations reflects this bias, promising dominion to those who uphold the law until his second coming.

St. John believed that the world's judgment day was imminent. In his vision, the Lamb breaks open seven seals, unleashing four horsemen—one with a crown, one with a sword, one with balances, and Death followed by Hell. God's martyrs receive white robes, and cosmic disturbances occur, with the sun darkening and the moon turning red.

An angel announces three woes on the earth, and four bound angels are released to wreak havoc. A conflict arises between a woman and a dragon, resulting in the dragon's defeat. Then, a beast with seven heads and ten horns emerges, and another beast creates an image to be worshipped, symbolizing the Roman Emperor Nero.

Despite temporary pagan dominance, the victorious Lamb stands on Mount Zion, heralding the preaching of the Gospel and the gathering of believers. Seven vials of wrath are poured out, leading to the downfall of Rome, depicted as Babylon. Satan is bound but later released for a final battle, culminating in the creation of a new heaven and earth.

The Revelation embodies early Jew-Christian views on God's plan and the struggle against evil. While Judaic Christianity faded, Rome became the hub of Gentile Christianity, exerting significant influence until the Reformation allowed for a more diverse and independent development of the faith.

St. John's Revelation portrays a vivid picture of impending judgment, with the Lamb breaking the seals and releasing four horsemen symbolizing conquest, war, famine, and death. Cosmic disturbances and angelic pronouncements of woe add to the apocalyptic imagery.

The struggle between good and evil is depicted through battles between heavenly forces and demonic entities, including a beast representing oppressive worldly powers. Despite temporary setbacks, the ultimate victory of righteousness is foretold, leading to the establishment of a new order and a heavenly Jerusalem.

This vision not only reflects the early Jew-Christian understanding of God's plan but also serves as a powerful commentary on the socio-political landscape of the time. While Judaic Christianity faded, Rome emerged as the epicenter of Gentile Christianity, shaping its trajectory until the era of the Reformation, which ushered in new dynamics and avenues for the faith's development.

The concept of Satan and Hell holds a significant place in early Christianity, with the belief that Christ, immediately after his crucifixion, descended into Hell and triumphed over the prince of darkness. Although the earliest versions of the Apostle's Creed lack the phrase "descended into hell," it was a widely accepted belief by the second century.

The Gospel of Nicodemus, likely from the third century, provides a detailed narrative of Christ's descent into Hell. It recounts Satan's conversation with the prince of hell, expressing fear and acknowledgment of Christ's divine power. Satan admits to his role in Christ's crucifixion but is fearful of facing Christ's might.

As the dialogue unfolds, a thunderous voice commands the gates of Hell to open for the King of Glory. The prince of hell, realizing Christ's power, commands Satan to leave and prepares to resist Christ's entry. However, the saints and prophets join in demanding the gates to open, citing prophecies of David.

Ultimately, Christ breaks through the gates of Hell, symbolizing victory over sin and death. This imagery underscores the belief in Christ's triumph and redemption, offering hope to believers.

After breaking through the gates of Hell, Christ liberates the souls held captive there, symbolizing redemption and salvation for humanity. This event is seen as a fulfillment of prophecy and a demonstration of God's power over sin and death.

The descent into Hell narrative underscores the significance of Christ's sacrifice and the ultimate victory of good over evil. It serves as a powerful symbol of hope and redemption for believers, emphasizing the transformative power of faith and the promise of eternal life.

Despite variations in interpretation and historical context, the story of Christ's descent into Hell remains a fundamental aspect of Christian theology, reminding believers of the profound depths of God's love and mercy.

"After this, the prophet Isaiah spoke to all the saints, saying, 'Didn't I prophesy rightly when I was alive on earth? The dead will live again, those in their graves will rise, and those in the earth will rejoice, for the dew from the Lord will bring deliverance to them. And elsewhere, I said, "O death, where is your victory? O death, where is your sting?"'

"When all the saints heard Isaiah's words, they urged the

prince of hell, 'Open your gates now and remove your iron bars, for you will now be bound and powerless.'

"Suddenly, a thunderous voice declared, 'Lift up your gates, O princes! Open, gates of hell, and the King of Glory will enter.'

"Confused, the prince of hell asked, 'Who is this King of Glory?' David responded, 'I understand the words of that voice, spoken through his spirit. The Lord is strong and mighty, the King of Glory, who hears the groans of the prisoners and sets free those appointed to death. Open your gates, foul prince of hell, for the King of Glory approaches.'

"As David spoke, the Lord appeared in human form, illuminating the darkness and breaking the unbreakable fetters. Death and her officers trembled as Christ appeared, realizing they were bound by him. They questioned his identity, marveling at his power and purity.

"The King of Glory, trampling death, seized the prince of hell, stripped him of power, and took Adam to glory.

"Addressing Satan, the prince of hell exclaimed, 'O prince of destruction, why did you crucify the innocent? You've lost all the sinners to us.'

"The King of Glory then told Beelzebub, 'Satan shall be subject to you forever, in place of Adam and his righteous sons.'

"Jesus reached out, saying, 'Come to me, all you saints, condemned by the devil and death. Live now by the wood of my cross; the devil is defeated, and death is conquered.'"

The saints rejoiced as they followed Jesus, freed from the grasp of death and sin. With Satan subdued and the prince of hell humbled, they embraced their newfound liberation. The power of the cross had triumphed, and the promise of eternal life shone brightly before them.

As they ascended with Christ, leaving behind the darkness of the underworld, they carried with them the hope and promise of redemption for all humanity. The victory over death was not just for them but for all who would believe in the power of Christ's sacrifice.

And so, in the light of this glorious triumph, the saints emerged from the depths of despair into the radiance of God's eternal love, forever grateful for the salvation wrought by the King of Glory.

The concept of Heaven and Hell among early Christians is vividly depicted in the Revelation of St. Peter. While not included in all early Christian texts, it was considered canonical by some, including Clement of Alexandria. The book was even read in churches in Palestine as part of Easter preparations in the 5th century.

In St. Peter's vision, Heaven is described as a place of radiant beauty and joy, where the righteous dwell in harmony, adorned in angelic robes, and surrounded by celestial splendor.

Conversely, Hell is portrayed as a grim and desolate realm of punishment. Those who blasphemed, perverted justice, or engaged in sinful acts find themselves in torment, hung by their tongues or engulfed in flames. Murderers face their victims, while adulterers and their accomplices endure agonizing trials. The damned suffer various tortures, from being devoured by worms to enduring fiery rays and scourging by evil spirits.

Women who committed abortions and those who bore

false witness face their own forms of punishment, as do the greedy and the idolaters. The torments of Hell are depicted as diverse and relentless, reflecting the severity of divine judgment upon those who have strayed from the path of righteousness.

St. Peter's vision serves as a stark reminder of the consequences of sin and the importance of leading a virtuous life according to the teachings of God.

Furthermore, St. Peter's revelation emphasizes the vivid imagery of Hell as a place of intense suffering and retribution for various sins. Those who engaged in acts of injustice, blasphemy, and moral corruption are depicted facing gruesome punishments tailored to their transgressions.

The vision includes scenes of torment for those who practiced adultery, murder, and deceit, as well as for the greedy and idolatrous. Each punishment is vividly described, illustrating the severity of divine judgment and the consequences of straying from the path of righteousness.

St. Peter's portrayal of Hell serves as a cautionary tale, warning believers of the eternal consequences of sin and urging them to lead lives guided by virtue and righteousness. It underscores the importance of moral integrity and fidelity to God's commandments to avoid the fate of damnation depicted in the vision.

Another depiction of Hell, according to the perspectives of third-century Christian Gnostics, can be found in the Pistis Sophia. This text provides a detailed account of the various regions of torment, offering insights into the beliefs of this particular Christian sect. Notably, the Pistis Sophia predates certain developments within the Catholic Church, emphasizing the importance of sacraments, mysteries, penance, and ascetic practices for salvation.

In the Pistis Sophia, Hell is referred to as the outer darkness, portrayed as a vast dragon surrounding the world. Within this dragon are twelve dungeons, each governed by a different ruler with a distinct appearance. The punishments inflicted in these dungeons vary, corresponding to the sins committed by the souls confined there.

The text describes the torment endured by blasphemers, adherents of false doctrines, those who engage in immoral behavior, and various other transgressors. Souls deemed unworthy are led into the outer darkness, where they face relentless suffering in icy conditions and scorching fires. The intensity of these torments far surpasses earthly judgments, with each dungeon offering its own unique horrors.

Despite the grim portrayal of Hell in the Pistis Sophia, the text also emphasizes the importance of repentance and spiritual redemption. However, those who persist in sin and reject the light-world are condemned to eternal damnation in the outer darkness.

While the doctrine of imminent judgment gradually faded as the Church gained power, depictions of the last judgment remained popular among Christian artists and poets. The concept of divine judgment and the impending end of the world continued to resonate within Christian theology, serving as a reminder of the consequences of sin and the need for moral rectitude.

The concept of Hell, as depicted in the Pistis Sophia, offers a glimpse into the beliefs of early Christian Gnostics, particularly those of the third century. This text, predating certain developments within the Catholic Church, provides a vivid description of the various regions of torment within the realm of the outer darkness.

In the Pistis Sophia, Hell is symbolized by a colossal dragon that envelops the world, with twelve dungeons contained within it. Each dungeon is ruled by a distinct entity, characterized by unique appearances and tasked with administering punishments corresponding to the sins committed by the souls therein.

The text outlines a variety of torments inflicted upon different categories of sinners, including blasphemers, adherents of false doctrines, and those who engage in immoral behavior. Souls deemed unworthy are led into the outer darkness, where they face unrelenting suffering in frigid ice and scorching fires. The intensity of these torments exceeds anything experienced in earthly judgments, emphasizing the severity of divine retribution.

Despite the grim portrayal of Hell, the Pistis Sophia also underscores the importance of repentance and spiritual redemption. However, those who persist in sin and reject the opportunity for salvation are consigned to eternal damnation in the outer darkness.

While the doctrine of imminent judgment may have waned as the Church gained influence, the notion of divine justice and the consequences of sin remained central to Christian theology. Depictions of the last judgment continued to resonate within Christian art and literature, serving as a reminder of the ultimate reckoning awaiting all souls.

The concept of Hell, as described in the Pistis Sophia, sheds light on the beliefs of early Christian Gnostics, particularly those in the third century. This text, predating certain developments within the Catholic Church, vividly illustrates the various realms of torment within what is termed the outer darkness.

In the Pistis Sophia, Hell is symbolized by a colossal dragon enveloping the world, within which are twelve dungeons. Each dungeon is governed by a distinct entity, characterized by unique appearances, responsible for administering punishments corresponding to the sins committed by the souls held within.

The text delineates a plethora of torments inflicted upon different categories of sinners, ranging from blasphemers to proponents of false doctrines and immoral behavior. Souls deemed unworthy are led into the outer darkness, where they endure relentless suffering in frigid ice and scorching fires. The severity of these torments surpasses anything experienced in earthly judgments, underscoring the gravity of divine retribution.

Despite the grim portrayal of Hell, the Pistis Sophia emphasizes the importance of repentance and spiritual redemption. However, those who persist in sin and spurn the opportunity for salvation are consigned to eternal damnation in the outer darkness.

While the belief in imminent judgment may have waned as the Church gained influence, the idea of divine justice and the consequences of sin remained pivotal to Christian theology. Depictions of the last judgment persisted in Christian art and literature, serving as a reminder of the ultimate reckoning awaiting all souls.

As Christianity evolved and gained prominence, the

understanding of Hell underwent transformations, reflecting diverse theological perspectives and cultural influences. One significant portrayal emerges from the Pistis Sophia, a text from the third century, providing insights into the beliefs of early Christian Gnostics.

In this intricate narrative, Hell is envisioned as a vast, engulfing dragon encircling the world, with twelve dungeons embedded within it. Each dungeon is overseen by a distinct ruler, each bearing a unique visage and administering punishments tailored to the sins of the damned.

The Pistis Sophia delves into the intricacies of these torments, detailing the suffering of souls condemned for various transgressions, from blasphemy to moral depravity. The vivid descriptions depict a realm of unfathomable anguish, where sinners endure relentless agony amidst freezing ice and scorching flames.

Despite its grim portrayal of divine retribution, the text also emphasizes the importance of repentance and redemption. Souls have the opportunity to seek salvation, but those who persist in wickedness face eternal condemnation in the outer darkness.

While the idea of imminent judgment may have diminished over time, the imagery of the last judgment persisted in Christian art and literature, serving as a potent reminder of the consequences of sin and the promise of divine justice.

As Christianity continued to evolve, the concept of Hell was explored through various theological lenses, offering diverse perspectives on the afterlife and divine punishment. One such exploration comes from the Pistis Sophia, a third-century text that sheds light on the beliefs of early Christian Gnostics.

In this intricate narrative, Hell is depicted as a colossal dragon enveloping the world, its twelve dungeons serving as chambers of torment for the damned. Each dungeon is presided over by a distinct ruler, each with a unique appearance and administering punishments tailored to the sins of the condemned.

The Pistis Sophia delves into the details of these punishments, painting a vivid picture of the suffering endured by souls condemned for their transgressions. From blasphemy to moral corruption, each sin is met with its own form of excruciating retribution, amidst icy cold and scorching flames.

While the text portrays a stark vision of divine judgment, it also underscores the possibility of redemption through repentance. However, those who persist in their wickedness face the bleak prospect of eternal condemnation in the outer darkness.

Although the notion of imminent judgment may have waned over time, the imagery of the last judgment remained a potent theme in Christian art and literature. It served as a reminder of the consequences of sin and the promise of divine justice, echoing through the ages as a cautionary tale.

Footnotes

1. "The end of the ages." This phrase is also referenced in Hebrews 9:26, where it mentions Christ's appearance occurring at the culmination of time.

2. Edited by Dr. Ed. Bratke, Bonn, 1891.

3. Referencing Romans 14 and 1 Corinthians 8.

4. Referring to Matthew 26:38.

5. Consult Harnack's work, "Fragments of the Gospel and Apocalypse of Peter," pages 5-6.

6. This quote is translated from Harnack's edition.

7. Further details are omitted intentionally.

8. See Harnack's "Texts and Studies," page 98.

9. Ibid., pages 94 and following.

10. These statements, like "Qui acceperit μυστήριον Ineffabilis, ille est ego" ("Whoever receives the mystery of the ineffable, that one is me") and others, indicate a connection to an older gnostic text or gospel, according to Harnack.

11. This description calls to mind the myths of the Midgard-serpent and foreshadows medieval depictions of Hell as a monstrous dragon.

12. The mention of "Ieou, the first man, the overseer of the light, the ancient of the first statue" echoes concepts found in the teachings of Simon Magus and other Gnostics, as well as the Adam of the Cabala.

13. In medieval depictions of Hell, souls are often shown being thrown into the open jaws of a dragon with pitchforks, displaying a grim sense of humor. The description of Hell in the Pistis Sophia appears to be more earnest in its portrayal.

14. An early representation of Dante's concept of an icy Hell.

11

THE IDEA OF
SALVATION IN
GREECE AND ITALY

Deliver us from evil. Matthew 6:14

The first century CE was marked by a growing concern about evil, leading to the establishment of religious
institutions aimed at reconciling sin and rescuing the soul
from the horrors of hell. Concepts like evil, sin, hell, salvation, and eternal life were prevalent in Greek culture even
before Plato, albeit intertwined with traditional mythology.
As Greek philosophers challenged the idolatry of polytheism,
a cultural shift occurred, paving the way for the emergence of
Christianity. This cultural shift, or perhaps more accurately,
the formation of the Christian Church, was a response to the
need to combat evil. In ancient times, fear of punishment

in the afterlife often led to practices like human sacrifice as a means of atonement. While these practices evolved over time, the underlying fear persisted, finding new expression in Christianity through the concept of Christ's sacrificial death. Christ's crucifixion, according to Pauline theology, was deemed sufficient for all future generations.

The ancient Greeks, like many other civilizations, dreaded post-mortem punishment above all else, and their belief in hell traces back to their earliest history.

The earliest depiction of the Greek underworld, found in Homer's works, shares similarities with the Jewish concept of Sheol, portraying Hades as the realm of the dead, encompassing both good and evil souls. It's depicted as a dismal place, featuring a grove of willow and poplar trees and a vast meadow covered in asphodel flowers. While early accounts don't mention rewards for the righteous (even the mighty Achilles faces the same fate as everyone else), they do describe various torments inflicted upon the wicked, such as Tantalus, the Danaids, Sisyphus, Ixion, and Oknos.

The idea of the afterlife and the fate of souls persisted throughout Greek mythology and culture, evolving over time as new beliefs and traditions emerged. As civilization progressed, so did the understanding of what awaited beyond death.

For the Greeks, the underworld was a realm shrouded in mystery and gloom, where shades of the deceased dwelled in a shadowy existence. However, this bleak vision of the after-life was not uniform across all Greek thought. Philosophers like Plato envisioned a more complex and nuanced realm of the dead, where souls faced judgment and underwent purification before potentially being reincarnated.

The fear of punishment in the afterlife, along with the hope for redemption and salvation, played a significant role in shaping Greek religious practices and beliefs. Sacrifices, rituals, and offerings were performed to appease the gods and ensure a favorable fate in the next life. The mysteries of death and the afterlife were explored in various myths, literature, and religious rites, reflecting the Greeks' profound fascination with the unknown.

Despite the diversity of beliefs and interpretations, the underlying fear of divine retribution and the desire for divine favor remained constant themes in Greek religion and culture. These concepts laid the groundwork for later religious developments, including the rise of Christianity, which would come to offer its own vision of salvation and redemption from the perils of the afterlife.

Homer's depiction of the dead in the underworld paints them as ethereal, almost like fleeting images in a dream. However, there are exceptions to this rule, such as Hercules, whose shadow resides in Hades while he himself, as an Immortal, dwells among the gods on Mount Olympus (as described in the Odyssey, XI., 601-626). Another figure with a more favorable fate in the afterlife is Menelaos. As the son-in-law of Zeus and husband to Helen, often associated with the moon goddess, he resides in Elysion under the rule of Rhadamanthys. Here, life is serene and tranquil, free from the harshness of snow, winter, and storms, with only gentle zephyrs blowing from the ocean.

The belief in Elysion finds its roots in Egyptian mythology, evident in the name Rhadamanthys, derived from Ra Amenthes, the divine ruler of the hidden realm of Amenti.

As Greek society transitioned towards adopting gnostic beliefs, ancient pagan myths underwent a transformation rather than outright abandonment. Hesiod's tale of the epic struggle between Zeus and the Titans echoes through the ages, while St. Peter, in his second letter, speaks of the rebellion of sinful angels cast down to Tartarus by God. However, in some translations like the King James Version, the term "Tartarus" is simply rendered as "hell," obscuring the original meaning.

This transformation of mythological narratives was part of a broader cultural shift as Greek society embraced gnostic perspectives, which laid the groundwork for the eventual adoption of Christianity. While ancient pagan myths persisted, they underwent reinterpretation rather than outright rejection.

Hesiod's Theogony, for instance, recounts the epic clash between Zeus and the Titans, a tale resonating with both historical and metaphorical significance. Similarly, St. Peter's second letter references the fall of rebellious angels, consigned to Tartarus by divine decree. However, in some translations like the King James Version, the nuanced term "Tartarus" is flattened into the generic term "hell," losing the specific mythological context.

As Greek culture evolved, these myths served as points of reference, adapting to fit new religious frameworks. This process of reinterpretation reflects the dynamic nature of belief systems, where older narratives are reimagined to accommodate evolving spiritual paradigms.

In Hesiod's Theogony, we encounter the epic confrontation between Zeus and the monstrous Typhon, also known as Typhoeus:

"When Zeus had vanquished the Titans and claimed dominion over heaven, the mighty Earth birthed her youngest son, Typhoeus. His hands boasted formidable strength, while atop his shoulders writhed a hundred serpentine heads with tongues of shadow. Fire blazed from his fearsome eyes, and from his cavernous mouths issued a cacophony of sounds, echoing the bellow of a bull, the roar of a lion, the bark of wild hounds, and the hiss of serpents. Typhoeus sought to reign over mortals until the father of gods and men intervened.

Zeus unleashed his thunderous fury, shaking Olympus and the earth beneath. The heavens and seas churned, and even the underworld quaked in dread. Tartarus, domain of the Titans, trembled. Yet Zeus subdued Typhoeus, scorching the monstrous heads with divine wrath. Beaten and crippled, the creature was cast into the abyss of Tartarus."

This clash mirrors the celestial battle depicted in Revelation 12:7-9, where Michael and his angels confront the dragon:

"And there was war in heaven. Michael and his angels fought against the dragon, and the dragon fought back, but he was defeated and cast down to earth. This dragon, the ancient serpent called the Devil and Satan, deceives the whole world, and he was hurled down with his angels."

In this way, the ancient Greek myths found resonance in early Christian texts, as the figures of old were recast to fit new narratives of spiritual warfare and redemption.

The stories of Perseus bear striking similarities to those

of Hercules. Like Hercules, Perseus is revered as a divine savior in Greek mythology. With the aid of Athena, he rescues Andromeda, symbolizing the bride of Death, from the clutches of the terrifying Medusa, an embodiment of mortal dread. The image of the Medusa's head, a potent symbol of vanquishing evil, frequently adorns shields and coins.

Another figure in this pantheon of heroes is Bellerophon, a solar champion who rides the winged horse Pegasus, representing the thundercloud, and slays the Chimera, a fearsome hybrid creature symbolizing barbarism and savagery.

Many of these tales of divine heroes may have roots in local Greek traditions, but they also bear the hallmarks of influences from the East, where ancient religions began shaping the beliefs of Western civilizations. Hercules, for instance, shares parallels with the Tyrian god Melkarth, likely synonymous with the Babylonian deity Bel, known for conquering chaos represented by Tiamat. Hercules' twelve labors align with the deeds of the sun-god throughout the twelve months of the year. Additionally, Hercules' demise and rebirth mirror the cyclical nature of the sun, symbolized by the phoenix rising from its own ashes. Even the Jewish tradition appropriates this solar archetype in the figure of Samson, whose strength lies in his hair, much like the sun's power in its rays.

Despite the infusion of foreign mythologies, Hercules endures as Greece's national hero, embodying the quintessential idea of salvation. This concept finds poignant expression in Aeschylus' tragedy, where Hercules rescues Prometheus, representing humanity's struggle, from torment at the hands of Zeus. This ancient tale resonates with the Christian narrative of Jesus Christ, who similarly overcomes suffering to deliver humanity from sin and death. In both cases, the hero's trials serve as tests of virtue and ultimately lead to spiritual victory over worldly temptations.

The concept of evil as hell found its philosophical underpinning in Plato's dualism, where he delves into its minutiae. His depiction of the soul's future state, with its heavenly rewards and punishments in hell, bears striking resemblance to Christian doctrines, albeit differing on the doctrine of soul transmigration.

Plato's Republic concludes with the tale of Er, who returns from death to impart knowledge about the afterlife. Er recounts a journey where souls face judgment and are directed either to ascend to heaven or descend to hell, bearing the symbols of their deeds. Hell is vividly portrayed as a place of torment, where sinners face retribution for their wrongs, a vision that predates Plato and resurfaces in various religious doctrines.

The rising and sinking of souls in hell, akin to Buddhagosha's parables, adds to the dread. Plato highlights the fear-driven rituals of expiation and atonement, perpetuated by mendicant prophets, who promise deliverance from hell's torment through sacrifices and rites.

Plato's dualistic views intensified in the Neo-Platonist movement and the Christian era, fostering a longing for death among philosophers and instilling fear among the populace. Callimachus satirically portrays this longing, attributing it to Plato's teachings on the soul.

The belief in hell, prevalent across cultures, engendered fear and sought salvation through various means, including

Christianity. Lucian's tale of Peregrinus, a convert who immolated himself, underscores the fervent religious zeal of the era.

Plutarch and others describe the haunting imagery of hell, feeding superstitious fears. The belief in hell, a primitive shadow cast across humanity, became a central tenet of Christianity, offering redemption from eternal damnation.

Early Christians, largely from humble backgrounds, absorbed influences from various traditions, including Platonic philosophy and Mithraic rites. Similarities between Christian sacraments and pagan practices were attributed to the cunning of Satan, yet these parallels predated Christianity itself.

The early Christians, predominantly from modest backgrounds, lacked extensive education and often lacked knowledge about the origins of their rituals. Platonic philosophy, if it entered their minds at all, did so indirectly through the works of figures like Philo. Consequently, they were often perplexed when confronted with similar practices and beliefs among non-Christians, attributing such parallels to the deceptive influence of Satan.

Even the central Christian sacrament, the Lord's Supper, had counterparts in other traditions. Justin Martyr noted similarities between Persian rituals and Christian practices, attributing these resemblances to demonic influence without hesitation. Tertullian similarly observed parallels between Church customs and the rites of Mithras worship, suggesting that Satan imitated divine sacraments.

These assertions may seem curious to modern sensibilities, but in the religious milieu of the time, where belief in supernatural forces was widespread, such explanations were plausible. The Devil, in the eyes of early Christians, appeared to be a cunning adversary, capable of anticipating and mimicking divine plans.

Ultimately, the fear of hell and the quest for salvation permeated many religious traditions, each offering its own path to redemption. Christianity, with its promise of deliverance from eternal damnation through the saving power of Christ's sacrifice, emerged as a compelling alternative amidst the diverse array of beliefs circulating in the ancient world.

Other religious movements of the time, seeking to encapsulate the spiritual ideals of the era, failed to gain traction against Christianity, which offered simplicity in its core beliefs and practical morality. However, the zealous fervor of Christian monks has largely erased the remnants of these competing religious aspirations, leaving behind only fragmentary evidence that is nonetheless intriguing to historians due to its similarities and differences with Christianity.

Among the competitors of Christianity were several Oriental deities who gained popularity in Rome, including Mithras, Serapis from Egypt, and Iao-Abraxas.

The influence of Mithras worship on Christianity is well-documented. Various rituals and beliefs, such as baptism, the Eucharist, facing east in prayer, sanctifying Sunday as the day of worship, and celebrating the winter solstice as the birth of the Savior, demonstrate this influence. For instance, the celebration of Christ's birth on December 25, originally the birthday of the Sun God Mithras, was a practice that evolved from the blending of Mithraism with Christianity.

Ancient inscriptions and Christian writings provide evidence of this syncretism. Early Christian authors like Ambrose and Chrysostom acknowledged the connection between the birthday of the Sun and the birth of Christ. Additionally, ancient Christian poets such as Prudentius and Paulinus of Nola made references to Christ's birth in connection with the changing of seasons.

While Christianity eventually became the dominant faith, remnants of pagan rituals persisted for centuries, as evidenced by a decree from a Roman council in 743 AD prohibiting the celebration of pagan rites on January 1. This indicates that even long after the decline of paganism, vestiges of these practices lingered within Christian communities.

Moreover, Christianity's appeal lay in its straightforward message and practical moral guidance, setting it apart from the more complex and esoteric teachings of its competitors. While other faiths attempted to embody the spiritual aspirations of the time, they often fell short, unable to resonate with people in the same way Christianity did.

The rise of Christianity also saw the decline of competing religions, with Mithraism being one of the most significant challengers. Mithraism, with its focus on rituals and symbolism, exerted a notable influence on early Christianity, particularly in the development of certain sacraments and religious practices.

For instance, the ritual of baptism, symbolic of spiritual purification and rebirth, was a practice shared by both Mithraism and Christianity. Similarly, the concept of the Eucharist, or communion, where believers partake in bread and wine as symbols of Christ's body and blood, bears resemblance to Mithraic rites involving sacred meals.

Facing east in prayer, sanctifying Sunday as a holy day, and even the timing of Christmas on December 25th, coinciding with the winter solstice and the birth of the unconquered sun in Mithraic tradition, all reflect the influence of Mithraism on early Christian practices.

While Christianity ultimately triumphed, absorbing and repurposing elements of other faiths along the way, traces of these religious syncretisms lingered for centuries. The blending of beliefs and practices from various traditions underscores the dynamic and evolving nature of religious expression throughout history.

In the religion of Mithras, Aeon, depicted as a lion-faced figure, holds significant importance. Aeon represents Zrvan Akarana, or Time Unlimited, in the Zend-avesta, symbolizing the primordial state of existence from which Ahura Mazda, the main deity, is born. Aeon is more of a personified abstraction than a distinct personality, embodying the concept of eternal time. The serpent coils around his body symbolize the cycles of time, while his wings represent the four seasons. Aeon's connection to Greek deities like Hephaestus, Asclepius, Hermes, and Dionysus is indicated by the presence of their emblems.

An interesting account from Flaminius Vacca describes the discovery of an Aeon statue. Found in a vineyard, the statue featured a lion's head atop a human body, with a globe under its feet and a serpent encircling it. The statue also had wings and keys in its hands, with lamps placed around it. While some interpreted it as symbolizing the Devil, others associated it with the ruler of all beasts.

Another deity, Iao, also known as Abraxas, is depicted with a cock's head, symbolizing healing. The serpent, representing mystery and wisdom, is depicted without feet, giving Iao serpent-legged features.

The Agathodaimon, or God of Goodness, is represented as a serpent with solar rays surrounding its head. This imagery was often found on gems and cylindrical boxes used in religious rituals.

The worship of Serapis, a Hellenized form of Osiris-Apis, bore resemblances to Christianity, with the cross as a sacred symbol. Serapis worshippers were even referred to as Christians by some. The similarities between Serapis cult practices and Christian monasticism in Egypt are notable.

Tot, or Tehuti, an Egyptian deity with an ibis head, symbolized divine cosmic order and was associated with the moon. In Greek mythology, Tot was identified with Hermes, revered as a savior figure and representative of divine wisdom.

Philosophers like Seneca, Epictetus, and Marcus Aurelius shared similarities with Christian teachings, advocating for morality and the fatherhood of God. However, they were more focused on philosophy than pastoral care.

Gnosticism posed a significant challenge to Christianity, with its dualistic views and emphasis on esoteric knowledge. Gnostic teachings often depicted the demiurge, identified with the Jewish Yahweh, as the creator of evil.

Manichaeism, founded by Manes, sought to synthesize various religious traditions but was considered heretical by mainstream Christianity.

Christianity incorporated pagan symbols and rituals, such as the use of statues, incense, and processions, into its practices. The labarum, interpreted as a monogram of Christ, and the cross became powerful religious symbols, believed to possess protective properties.

Saints like St. George and St. Michael were depicted as warriors battling evil forces, reflecting the warlike spirit prevalent in Christianity.

Despite Jesus' teachings of peace, later Christians embraced a belligerent ethos influenced by pagan traditions, particularly among the energetic northern races.

The veneration of saints like St. Anthony of Egypt, who was said to have engaged in fierce battles with demons in the desert, further perpetuated the idea of spiritual warfare within Christianity. These accounts, recorded by Bishop Athanasius, became popularized and depicted in dramatic artworks, such as Salvator Rosa's painting of St. Anthony's struggle against the devil.

While Jesus' original teachings emphasized peace and non-resistance to evil, the incorporation of pagan motifs and the influence of belligerent cultures led to a shift in Christian attitudes towards warfare and spiritual combat. The conversion of energetic northern nations, like the Norsemen and Anglo-Saxons, brought a martial spirit into Christianity, albeit tempered with qualities of strength, generosity, fairness, and moral purity.

Despite the initial peaceful ethos of Jesus' teachings, Christianity evolved to encompass elements of spiritual struggle and the valorization of warrior saints. This transformation reflects the complex interplay between religious doctrine, cultural influences, and historical context in shaping the beliefs and practices of Christian communities over time.

The evolving nature of Christianity incorporated elements

of spiritual conflict and the exaltation of warrior saints along-side its original emphasis on peace. This shift illustrates the dynamic interplay between religious teachings, cultural influences, and historical context. As Christianity spread among northern European nations like the Norsemen and Anglo-Saxons, it encountered societies with a strong martial tradition. Consequently, the faith adopted aspects of valor and spiritual warfare, which found expression in the veneration of saints like St. Anthony of Egypt.

Accounts of St. Anthony's confrontations with demons, as chronicled by Bishop Athanasius and depicted in artworks such as Salvator Rosa's paintings, became popularized. These tales reflected a belief in the ongoing struggle between good and evil, with saints like St. Anthony serving as exemplars of spiritual combat. However, this narrative of conflict coexisted with Jesus' original teachings of peace and nonviolence.

Over time, Christianity adapted to incorporate diverse cultural practices and beliefs, including those related to warfare and heroism. This adaptation allowed the faith to resonate with various communities while maintaining its core principles. Thus, while the early Christian doctrine emphasized pacifism, subsequent developments introduced a more complex understanding of spiritual struggle and the role of saints as warriors against evil forces.

As Christianity continued to evolve, it encountered diverse cultural traditions and beliefs, leading to a complex intermingling of spiritual concepts. One notable aspect of this evolution was the incorporation of elements related to spiritual conflict and the veneration of warrior saints.

St. George, revered as a patron saint of fighters,

exemplifies this fusion of martial prowess and Christian devotion. Legends surrounding St. George depict him as a valiant knight who bravely confronted a dragon terrorizing a pagan city. Through his courageous actions, St. George not only vanquished the dragon but also converted the city's inhabitants to Christianity. While historical accounts paint a different picture of St. George as an archbishop of Alexandria with no heroic deeds to his name, the legend of his dragon-slaying exploits captured the imagination of believers, symbolizing the triumph of good over evil.

Similarly, the Archangel Michael emerged as a prominent figure in Christian iconography, depicted as a celestial warrior vanquishing Satan and weighing souls on the day of judgment. This imagery drew parallels with ancient mythological tales of gods battling cosmic adversaries, reflecting the blending of Christian theology with cultural motifs of heroism and conflict.

The narratives of saints like St. Anthony of Egypt further underscored the theme of spiritual warfare, portraying them as courageous defenders against demonic forces. These accounts, often embellished with dramatic encounters and miraculous interventions, served to inspire believers and reinforce the notion of a cosmic struggle between good and evil.

While the early teachings of Jesus emphasized peace and nonviolence, the subsequent incorporation of warrior saints and tales of spiritual combat reflected Christianity's adaptation to diverse cultural contexts and human experiences. This dynamic evolution allowed the faith to resonate with believers across different societies while retaining its core message of love, compassion, and redemption.

Footnotes:

1. Throughout Christian history, there has been a consistent belief in the necessity of a human sacrifice to atone for sin. This idea is rooted in the mystical power of faith, with Christ's death on the cross often likened to Abraham's offering of Isaac and the miraculous healing brought about by the brazen serpent in the desert.

2. Alternatively, it should be noted that the authorship of the second epistle of St. Peter is attributed to another individual.

3. These references are found in Xenophon's "Memorabilia" and Plato's "Symposium."

4. Trendelenburg interprets a passage from Achilles Tatius, suggesting that it describes a scene resembling the myth of Andromeda. In this interpretation, Andromeda, depicted as a bride of death, is bound to two poles while Cupid oversees wedding preparations. Cassiopeia, Andromeda's mother, and other figures are also depicted, along with Perseus fighting the monster.

5. The Greek word "καλός" encompasses more than just the idea of beauty as commonly understood.

6. The Medusa, referenced by Homer as a fearsome underworld monster, was often used as an amulet for protection against evil. It later became a popular motif on shields, as seen in the illustration from the Acropolis at Athens.

7. The statue depicted on page 208 predates the

conventional portrayal of Pegasus with wings. The association of Pegasus with poetic inspiration emerged much later, in the fifteenth century, and was not part of the original Greek conception.

8. Images of a savior figure slaying a lion are also found on coins from Asia and on Assyrian cylinders.

9. The sarcophagus illustrated on page 212 depicts the myth of Prometheus, although the initial depiction of Prometheus stealing fire seems incomplete.

10. The case of Cleombrotus, a disciple of Socrates who committed suicide, is referenced in Plato's "Phaedo" and later alluded to by St. Augustine in "The City of God."

11. Referring back to page 210 for further information.

12. The gemstone described here, likely given as a Christian New Year's gift, depicts the death of a martyr. The letters "ANFT" stand for "annum novum felicem tibi."

13. This passage refers to the Apology and Acts of Apollonius, as translated by F. C. Conybeare in "Monuments of Early Christianity."

14. Other references to the Mithras cult can be found in the writings of Justin Martyr and Tertullian. The cult, popular among Roman soldiers in the northern provinces, involved initiation rituals and beliefs in Mithras as a mediator for the forgiveness of sins.

15. The Mithras mysteries, introduced into Greece during Alexander the Great's time, gained significant influence in the second century CE, with numerous monuments found throughout the Roman Empire, particularly in Gaul and Germany.

16. Various inscriptions and writings mention the worship

of Mithras alongside invocations to the sun and moon, reflecting syncretic religious practices.

17. The passages quoted from Chrysostom highlight the adoption of December 25th as Christ's birthday, possibly to coincide with the birth of Mithras, allowing Christians to practice their rites without interference.

18. Chrysostom's writings also illustrate how some individuals celebrated December 25th not only as Christ's birthday but also as a symbol of the renewal of the sun.

19. Similarly, other authors and poets connected Christ's birth with the increasing light of the sun after the winter solstice.

20. Historically, there were objections to celebrating January 1st and the Brumalia festival due to their association with pagan rituals.

21. The statue depicted on page 225 was found in the Mithraeum of Ostia and represents Mithras slaying a bull, a significant motif in Mithraic iconography.

22. The term "Abraxas" likely originates from Egyptian language and represents a deity to be adored, as evidenced by its presence in Biblical references.

23. Another gemstone inscription references the Good Spirit and the Eternal Sun, suggesting syncretism between different religious traditions.

24. The term "Pymander" is often interpreted to mean "shepherd of man," reflecting divine guidance.

25. The equilateral cross, frequently adorned with four dots, likely symbolizes the sun in its various positions, as seen in Egyptian depictions and Greek deity attire.

26. For further exploration of the history and significance

of the cross, readers are referred to the author's articles in The Open Court.

27. Egyptian monuments depict the use of the cross as an amulet worn around the neck, similar to its usage in Greece.

28. The illustration on page 238 depicts a Mithraic ritual, likely involving a baptism or initiation ceremony.

29. These individuals, better known to God than to humans, likely refer to devout believers or martyrs.

30. For more information on St. Anthony, readers are directed to the Acta Sanctorum of the Bolandists for January 17th and Latin translations of St. Anthony's letters found in the Biblioteca Patrum.

12

THE DEMONOLOGY OF NORTHERN EUROPE

The religion of the Teutons was primarily centered around the ethos of warriors. They believed that life itself was a constant struggle, and thus, courage was seen as the foundation of all virtue. Rather than shying away from conflict, they embraced it, facing challenges head-on with unwavering bravery. Their principal deity was the god of war, and they revered death on the battlefield as the highest achievement. They held in contempt those who feared wounds and death, instead valuing honesty, bravery, and integrity in combat.

The concept of evil played a significant role in Teutonic religion, embodied by Loki, the mischievous god of fire.

According to legend, Loki introduced sin and wickedness into the world, leading to various calamities and misfortunes. He deceived the gods on multiple occasions, orchestrating treacherous schemes that resulted in chaos and tragedy. His most notorious act was the death of Baldur, the god of light and purity, which led to his banishment from the realm of the gods.

One of the most striking aspects of Teutonic mythology is the idea of Ragnarok, or the twilight of the gods, symbolizing the final destruction of the world and its deities. This cataclysmic event, foretold in prophecy, marks the ultimate showdown between the forces of good and evil, culminating in the annihilation of both. Yet, from the ashes of this devastation, a new world will emerge, brighter and better than before, inhabited by a new race of beings.

When Christianity spread to Northern Europe, it encountered the Teutonic peoples, who infused their own beliefs and traditions into the Christian framework. As a result, Christianity took on distinctly Teutonic characteristics, with Christ depicted as a warrior king and the disciples as loyal vassals. Even pagan festivals were adapted into Christian celebrations, such as Yuletide becoming Christmas. Moreover, Teutonic concepts of evil, embodied by figures like Loki, were assimilated into Christian demonology, shaping popular notions of hell and demonic entities.

The influence of Northern mythology on Christian thought is evident in various aspects, including the themes of death and resurrection, judgment day, and the renewal of the world. While Christianity originated in the East, the idea of a dying and resurrected god finds its roots in Northern traditions, highlighting the cultural exchange and synthesis that occurred between different belief systems over time.

Dr. Ernst Krause, writing under the pseudonym Carus Sterne, delved into the influence of Northern folklore on Southern fairy tales and legends. He proposed that myths depicting the death and rebirth of the sun, symbolizing immortality and the cyclical nature of life, originated in Northern regions where the return of sunlight on Christmas Day represented a renewal of light and vitality. These themes, echoed in legends of doomsday and the eventual restoration of the world, illustrate the deep-seated cultural beliefs that transcended geographical boundaries.

While scholars often draw parallels between the Nibelungenlied and Homer's epics, Krause suggests that the origins of the Nibelungenlied may predate those of Homer, with its themes of cosmic destruction and renewal found in the Völuspa, the first poem of the Norse Edda. This vision of an apocalyptic event, predating Christ's prophecies of judgment, underscores the enduring influence of Northern mythology on Christian ideas of eschatology and redemption.

In summary, Christianity, while originating in the East, underwent a process of "Teutonisation" as it spread across Northern Europe. The fusion of Teutonic beliefs with Christian doctrine resulted in a uniquely Northern interpretation of Christianity, characterized by a warrior ethos, a vivid demonology, and a cyclical understanding of time and salvation. This cultural exchange between Christianity and Northern folklore demonstrates the dynamic nature of religious thought and its ability to adapt and evolve in response to different cultural contexts.

Dr. Krause asserts that Dante's vivid portrayal of hell in the "Divina Commedia," a cornerstone of Roman Catholic Christian belief, draws heavily from Northern European mythology. Dante's vision of hell, characterized by wintry desolation rather than fiery torment, reflects the influence of Teutonic traditions that were widespread in Christian Europe during his time. This depiction of an icy hell, reminiscent of the desolate landscapes of Northern Europe, suggests a deep-rooted Northern influence on the concept of hell that may trace back to ancient Gnostic beliefs.

Dante's portrayal of Satan and hell reflects not just his own imagination but also incorporates numerous old traditions. His depiction of hell draws parallels with various myths and legends, including Knight Owain's descent into St. Patrick's Purgatory in Ireland and accounts of hell described by earlier Christian writers like Beda, Albericus, and Chevalier Tundalus. In Dante's narrative, Satan's abode is shrouded in thick fog and surrounded by icy blizzards, evoking imagery akin to the harsh landscapes of Northern Europe.

Moreover, Dante's description of Satan, referred to as "Dis," bears resemblance to the principal deity of evil in Northern European mythology, with three faces representing different aspects of darkness and malevolence. This imagery mirrors the trinity concept found in pagan beliefs, such as the Slavic deity Triglaf, whose three faces symbolize various attributes of evil.

The transformation of Teutonic giants into Christian

devils is another intriguing aspect of this cultural exchange. In Northern mythology, giants symbolized the raw forces of nature and were often outwitted by gods or humans through cunning and wisdom. Legends of heroism, like that of Beowulf battling the giant Grendel and his mother, reflect humanity's struggle against the primordial forces of nature personified by these giants.

Overall, Dante's "Divina Commedia" serves as a testament to the complex interplay between Christian doctrine and Northern European mythology, illustrating how cultural exchanges shape religious beliefs and narratives over time.

In addition to Dante's "Divina Commedia," which heavily draws from Northern European mythology, other significant cultural and religious shifts occurred as Christianity spread across Northern Europe. The fusion of Christian doctrine with Teutonic and Celtic traditions resulted in a unique blend of beliefs and narratives.

One notable transformation was the adaptation of pagan giants into Christian demons. In Northern mythology, giants represented natural forces and were often depicted as adversaries of gods or humans. As Christianity took root in the region, these ancient figures were reimagined as malevolent beings opposed to divine order. Stories of heroism, such as Beowulf's battles against giants, evolved to reflect humanity's struggle against evil forces, now personified as demonic entities.

Furthermore, the concept of hell underwent a profound reinterpretation influenced by Northern European imagery. While classical depictions often portrayed hell as a fiery realm of torment, Northern traditions favored desolate, wintry landscapes. Dante's vision of hell in "Divina Commedia," with its icy expanses and freezing winds, reflects this Northern influence. The portrayal of Satan as a three-faced entity, reminiscent of pagan deities like Triglaf, further underscores the blending of Christian theology with Northern mythological motifs.

This cultural exchange also extended to Christian demonology and folklore. Stories featuring the Devil and demonic entities incorporated elements of Northern legends, enriching Christian narratives with themes of struggle and triumph over evil. The integration of Northern imagery, such as frost giants and foggy marshes, into Christian demonology contributed to a rich tapestry of beliefs and stories.

Overall, the encounter between Christianity and Northern European traditions resulted in a dynamic exchange of ideas and symbols. Through this process, ancient myths and legends found new expression within Christian theology, shaping the religious landscape of medieval Europe and beyond.

As Christianity spread across Northern Europe, it encountered rich traditions and mythologies deeply rooted in the region's culture. This collision of faiths led to a fascinating exchange, where Christian beliefs merged with indigenous narratives, resulting in a complex tapestry of religious ideas and symbols.

One notable outcome of this interaction was the transformation of pagan giants into Christian demons. In Northern mythology, giants symbolized natural forces and often served as adversaries to gods and humans alike. With the advent of Christianity, these ancient figures were re-imagined as malevolent beings opposing divine order. Stories of heroism, such as the epic battles depicted in sagas like Beowulf, took on new meaning as allegories of humanity's struggle against evil forces, now personified as demonic entities.

Moreover, the concept of hell underwent a significant reinterpretation influenced by Northern European imagery. While classical depictions portrayed hell as a fiery inferno, Northern traditions favored desolate, wintry landscapes. Dante's portrayal of hell in his "Divine Comedy," featuring icy expanses and freezing winds, reflects this Northern influence. The depiction of Satan as a three-faced entity, reminiscent of pagan deities like Triglaf, further underscores the fusion of Christian theology with Northern mythological motifs.

This cultural exchange also extended to Christian demonology and folklore. Stories featuring the Devil and demonic entities incorporated elements of Northern legends, enriching Christian narratives with themes of struggle and triumph over evil. The integration of Northern imagery, such as frost giants and foggy marshes, into Christian demonology contributed to a diverse array of beliefs and stories.

Overall, the encounter between Christianity and Northern European traditions led to a dynamic blending of ideas and symbols. Through this process, ancient myths and legends found new expression within Christian theology, shaping the religious landscape of medieval Europe and beyond.

The grand processions of towering figures that grace Dutch and Flemish festivals might trace their roots to ancient customs symbolizing the visits of landowners collecting their dues. In these lively spectacles, the locals chant the refrain of the giant-song, urging the colossal figures to "Return once more, little giant."

Another dark tradition linked to the belief in natural forces owning the land was the practice of burying alive. This grim custom stemmed from the idea of offering sacrifices to appease powerful and malevolent landlords of the earth. Sacrifices, whether of humans or animals, were deemed necessary to fulfill the debt owed to these super-natural landowners.

Historical accounts and folklore abound with tales of this barbaric practice. Foundations of buildings were believed to require living creatures, even humans, entombed within them as sacrifices to ensure the stability and longevity of the structures. Such stories persisted, with some even gaining religious sanction, despite the moral teachings of Christian-ity.

Instances are cited where even Christian authorities, in their ignorance, endorsed such practices. In some cases, the construction of churches was believed to necessitate these cruel sacrifices, with priests sometimes being buried alive in particularly sacred sites.

The remnants of these superstitions endured long after the actual practice had ceased, underscoring the powerful grip of ancient beliefs on society's psyche.

The persistence of these superstitions well into more enlightened times is remarkable. Even as society evolved and

Christianity spread, remnants of these ancient beliefs clung tenaciously to cultural consciousness.

In 1813, during the repair of a dam on the river Elbe, an elderly man insisted to the dike-inspector that the repairs would never hold unless they buried an innocent child within the dam's foundation. Similarly, in 1843, during the construction of a new bridge in Halle, rumors circulated that a child must be interred in the bridge's structure for its stability.

Such instances illustrate how deeply ingrained these beliefs were, transcending the boundaries of religion and logic. Even in cases where Christianity should have dispelled such notions, they persisted, upheld by ignorance and fear.

The Strasbourg cathedral, an iconic symbol of faith and architecture, stands as a chilling example. Legend has it that the construction of this sacred edifice required the sacrifice of two human lives, with two brothers buried alive in its foundation.

These tales serve as haunting reminders of humanity's darker impulses and the enduring power of superstition in shaping history. Despite our advancements and enlightenment, the echoes of ancient fears still reverberate in the annals of our past.

The parades featuring giant families that are a prominent aspect of Dutch and Flemish carnivals might trace back to older customs symbolizing the visits of landowners collecting their dues. During these parades, refreshments are offered as homage, accompanied by the singing of the giant-song with the recurring line: "Keer u eens om, reuzjen,

reuzjen!" which translates to "Return once more little giant, little giant."

The notion of forces of nature, whether they be gods, demons, or giants, holding the privilege of collecting rent led to the superstition of burying alive either humans or animals. This practice, nearly universal at a certain stage of civilization, even found its way into religious sanction, including in the Old Testament.

In more recent history, superstitions surrounding the necessity of burying sacrifices within the foundation of structures persisted. In the 19th century, during the repair of a dam on the river Elbe and the construction of a new bridge in Halle, there were rumors that an innocent child had to be interred within these structures for stability.

Even with the advent of Christianity and the spread of enlightenment, remnants of these ancient beliefs lingered. Legends abound, such as the tale of the Strasbourg cathedral, which allegedly required the sacrifice of two human lives during its construction, serving as a chilling reminder of humanity's capacity for superstition and its enduring influence on culture and history.

The tales of outsmarting evil, whether it be giants or devils, are woven into the folklore of many cultures. In Germany, the landscape is dotted with large boulders, said to be remnants of giants' or devils' rage, either dropped as they stormed off in anger or shaken loose from their shoes. One tale recounts a farmer's cleverness in dividing his crops with the Devil, offering him the choice of the upper or lower half, only to outwit him with a strategic choice of crops, leaving the Devil with the less desirable share.

Similar stories can be found in Arabian folklore, where the Devil is also outwitted by cunning mortals. Friedrich Rückert retold one such tale in his poem "The Devil Outwitted," recounting how Arab farmers tricked the Devil into taking the less valuable portion of their crops.

Legends of foolish devils abound, from a miller who tied the Devil to a water-wheel to a tailor who terrorized demons with his sewing tools. Even saints had their encounters with the Devil, with St. Dunstan famously grabbing him by the nose with red-hot tongs and St. Cuthbert intervening to save a child from demonic clutches.

These stories, steeped in Christian imagery, reflect humanity's enduring fascination with the battle between good and evil. Whether through cleverness, divine intervention, or sheer bravery, these tales offer insights into the human psyche and our quest for redemption and salvation.

The tradition of human sacrifice to appease the forces of nature, whether gods, demons, or giants, is deeply rooted in ancient cultures and has left its mark on folklore and superstition. Even as civilizations progressed, remnants of this practice persisted, sometimes sanctioned even by religious authorities.

Legends abound of builders burying living creatures or even humans within the foundations of great structures, believing this act would ensure stability and longevity. Despite the moral teachings of Christianity, such practices endured, often justified in the name of faith.

One tale recounts the sinking walls of Copenhagen, only stabilized after the sacrifice of an innocent child. Similar stories emerged across Europe, from Scutari to Halle, where communities believed that burying individuals alive would secure the success of their projects.

Even churches were not exempt from these superstitions. According to some accounts, the construction of sacred buildings required sacrificial offerings, with priests or other holy figures sometimes deemed necessary for the task.

These beliefs persisted long after the cessation of actual human sacrifices, highlighting the enduring power of super-stition and the complex interplay between religion and tradition. The legends serve as a reminder of humanity's capacity for both faith and folly, and the ways in which our past shapes our present beliefs and practices.

Another aspect of folklore portrays clever individuals outsmarting malevolent entities, whether demons, devils, or giants. These tales often feature ordinary people using wit and cunning to overcome supernatural adversaries.

In one story, a farmer outwits the Devil, who demands a share of the crops from newly cultivated land. The farmer cleverly offers the Devil his choice of the upper or lower half of the harvest. Regardless of the Devil's choice, the farmer manipulates the situation to ensure that the Devil receives the less desirable portion.

Similar stories abound in various cultures, demonstrating humanity's fascination with narratives of cleverness triumphing over evil. These tales often serve as cautionary fables, encouraging listeners to rely on their intelligence and resourcefulness in navigating life's challenges.

Moreover, these stories reflect a universal theme of the underdog prevailing against seemingly insurmountable odds. Whether facing supernatural foes or everyday obstacles,

individuals who employ cunning and ingenuity are celebrated as heroes in these timeless tales.

In another folklore motif, individuals exploit the weaknesses of malevolent beings, such as demons or devils, to
gain the upper hand. These tales often highlight the human
capacity for outsmarting and overcoming even the most
formidable adversaries through cleverness and resourcefulness.

One such story features a miller who devises a cunning
plan to thwart the Devil's mischief. By tying the Devil to the
water-wheel of his mill, the miller prevents him from
causing harm or wreaking havoc in the community. This act
of bravery not only protects the miller and his neighbors but
also demonstrates the power of human ingenuity in out-
witting supernatural threats.

Similarly, a blacksmith who receives a wish from a divine
entity uses his newfound power to trick the Devil. By
bewitching the Devil and placing him on his anvil, the blacksmith intimidates the fearsome creature into submission,
ensuring that he and his community remain safe from harm.

These stories serve as reminders of the human capacity
for cleverness and resourcefulness in the face of adversity.
They inspire listeners to approach challenges with creativity
and ingenuity, knowing that even the most daunting
obstacles can be overcome through wit and determination.

Footnotes:

1. "Die Trojaburgen Nord-Europas." Published by Carl
Flemming in Glogau in 1893.

2. Reported in Vossische Zeitung, 1896, February 2, 9, 10; Sonntagsbeilagen.

3. Floegel's "Geschichte des Grotesk-Komischen," cited in Ebeling, page 286, quotes the giant-song as sung in Ypern.

4. Referencing I Book of Kings, chapter 16, verse 34.

5. Various sources including Grimm's Märchen, Deutsche Mythologie, Müllenhoff, and Thiele's Dänische Sagen, among others.

6. "Der betrogene Teufel."

7. Preusker's "Blicke in die vaterländische Vorzeit," Volume I, page 182.

8. Mentioned in Grimm's Märchen.

9. Translated by the author. The song can be found in various collections of German folk-songs. The first verse goes:

"A tailor went to wander,
On Monday, in the morn,
And there he met the Devil,
His clothes and shoes all torn.
Hey, hey, you tailor friend,
You must come with me, no end,
For you shall dress the devils,
Whatever it may cost."

10. Referenced in Grimm's Deutsche Sagen, 336, and Tobler's Appenzeller Sprachschatz, 214.

13

THE DEVIL'S PRIME

There's an old Latin saying: "Si duo faciunt idem, non est idem" (if two do the same thing, it is not the same thing), and this holds true not just for individuals, but also for nations and religions. It's common for people to overlook the faults of their own group while being critical of others. For instance, what the priests of Pharaoh and Moses did—performing tricks similar to those of modern snake charmers in Egypt and India—was seen as miraculous only when Moses did it, not when the priests did. The same applies to other religious figures throughout history.

The early Christians, like some Gnostics and other groups, practiced healing through prayer and laying on of hands, but today's churches don't endorse faith healing or Christian science.

Old accusations against Christians, like those made by the early Roman writer Tacitus, portrayed them negatively, just as Christians often ridiculed pagan beliefs. The truth is often somewhere in between, with both sides exaggerating the faults of the other.

In many ancient cultures, there was a belief in magic and the supernatural. The desire for miracles and the supernatural often arose from a dualistic worldview, where natural means were insufficient to achieve certain ends. Miracles were seen as legitimate if performed by one's own religion, but as witchcraft if done by others. This double standard persists today in different forms.

The belief in magic and miracles has been a natural part of human evolution, giving rise to practices like rain dances among Native American tribes and other rituals aimed at divine intervention. These practices show a deep spiritual devotion, much like that seen in ancient religious communities.

In the evolution of human societies, the belief in miracles and magic has been a significant aspect, often tied to the yearning for the attainment of goals beyond what natural means could achieve. This belief manifests in various forms across cultures and religions, serving as a testament to the human quest for understanding and control over the unknown.

Throughout history, different cultures have attributed supernatural powers to individuals or groups within their own religious or cultural framework. For instance, practices such as rain dances among Native American tribes or rituals aimed at invoking divine intervention are seen as legitimate expressions of faith and devotion within those communities.

However, when similar acts are performed by those outside of one's own religious or cultural sphere, they are often viewed with suspicion or even condemned as witchcraft or heresy. This double standard reflects the tendency of human societies to uphold their own beliefs while dismissing or denigrating those of others.

In contemporary society, while the belief in miracles and magic may have waned in some respects due to advancements in science and technology, it still persists in various forms. For example, faith healing and spiritual practices continue to have followers who believe in their efficacy, even in the face of skepticism or criticism from others.

Ultimately, the belief in miracles and magic speaks to a fundamental aspect of human nature—the desire to transcend the limitations of the natural world and connect with something greater than ourselves. Whether through religious rituals, mystical experiences, or other spiritual practices, humans continue to seek meaning and purpose in the mysteries of existence.

Any religion or spiritual practice that promises worldly success and claims to achieve salvation through miracles, whether performed by its founders or institutionalized through rituals like sacraments, pilgrimages, or mass readings, can be considered a form of magic. Essentially, a religion of magic relies on the belief in supernatural intervention, and once it becomes established, it typically distinguishes its own miracles from those of outsiders, labeling the latter as witchcraft.

To illustrate this concept, consider the writings of Agrippa of Nettesheim, a prominent philosopher of the Reformation era. Agrippa advocated for what he called "natural" or "celestial" magic, which he believed could lead to a profound union with the divine. His work, "De Occulta Philosophia," explores the idea of using magic to manipulate emotions, control weather, and achieve various other extraordinary feats through a mystical connection with God. Despite the similarities between Agrippa's magic and the alleged practices of witches, he faced little opposition at the time, as his views were widely accepted.

Agrippa's blend of occultism with scientific observation, as seen in his chapter on "The Proportions of the Human Body," reflects a fascinating combination of mathematics, natural science, and mysticism. However, Agrippa eventually became disillusioned with the concept of magic, realizing that it offered no real solutions. His skepticism extended to science itself, leading him to question the possibility of knowledge.

In essence, a religion of magic inevitably entails a belief in witchcraft. When sacraments are used as tools for extraordinary feats, any attempt to wield supernatural powers outside the established religious framework is often viewed as heresy. Thus, the connection between heresy and witchcraft arises from the belief that only the sanctioned authorities possess the ability to access the supernatural realm.

This association between heresy and witchcraft persists because any divergence from the established religious practices is often perceived as a challenge to authority. In religious systems where sacraments are considered powerful tools for spiritual intervention, the notion of performing miracles outside of this framework is seen as a breach of loyalty. Consequently, any unauthorized attempt to access the supernatural realm, regardless of the intentions behind it, is condemned as witchcraft.

Agrippa's exploration of celestial magic exemplifies this tension between sanctioned and unsanctioned supernatural practices. Despite his philosophical inquiries and attempts to reconcile mysticism with scientific observation, his ideas ultimately clashed with established religious doctrines. His disillusionment with magic eventually led him to question the very foundations of knowledge and science, highlighting the inherent complexities and uncertainties surrounding beliefs in the supernatural.

In summary, the intertwining of religion, magic, and witchcraft reflects a broader societal struggle to define and control access to the supernatural realm. As individuals and institutions grapple with questions of authority and legitimacy, the boundaries between sanctioned miracles and forbidden magic blur, shaping perceptions of heresy and witchcraft within religious communities.

The connection between heresy and witchcraft endures because any deviation from established religious norms is often viewed as a threat to authority. In religious traditions where sacraments hold significant spiritual power, any attempt to perform miracles outside of these rituals is seen as disloyalty. Consequently, any unauthorized pursuit of supernatural phenomena, regardless of intent, is condemned as witchcraft.

Agrippa's exploration of celestial magic illustrates this tension between accepted and unauthorized mystical practices. Despite his efforts to blend mysticism with scientific inquiry, his ideas clashed with established religious beliefs. His disillusionment with magic ultimately led him to question the very basis of knowledge and science, revealing the complexities and uncertainties surrounding beliefs in the supernatural.

In essence, the intersection of religion, magic, and witchcraft reflects a broader societal struggle to define and regulate access to the supernatural realm. As individuals and institutions grapple with questions of authority and legitimacy, the lines between sanctioned miracles and forbidden magic become blurred, shaping perceptions of heresy and witchcraft within religious communities.

Belief in Witchcraft: A Dark Chapter in Human History

The era of witchcraft belief marks a significant shift in human development. During this time, the Devil rose to prominence, reaching the zenith of his influence. Contracts with the Devil were purportedly made, with individuals trading their souls for various favors.

By the 13th century, the Devil's sway was undeniable. Every unusual event was attributed to him, and even mundane occurrences were seen as his handiwork. He was depicted in various forms, from animals to humans, embodying different roles in society.

Works like Gervasius Tilberiensis's "Otia Imperialia" and Cæsarius von Heisterbach's "Dialogus Miraculorum" perpetuated these beliefs. Cæsarius's writings, in particular, reflected the prevailing mindset of the time, portraying the Devil as a constant threat.

The fear of witchcraft permeated society, influencing even the clergy. Tales of demonic possession and supernatural encounters were widespread, further fueling the paranoia.

However, not everyone succumbed to these superstitions. Some sought to exploit them, like Christian Elsenreiter, who sold fake charms for protection. Others, like Saxon Colonel, believed in the power of objects like Mansfeld-Thalers to ward off harm.

Magic and divination practices flourished, with people using various methods to predict the future or locate hidden treasures. Horoscopes and conjurations were commonplace, offering glimpses into what lay ahead.

Yet, amidst the darkness, there were moments of clarity. Individuals like Galileo Galilei challenged the prevailing beliefs, risking persecution to champion scientific inquiry. As the Enlightenment dawned, the grip of witchcraft belief began to loosen, paving the way for a more rational understanding of the world.

In the end, it was the light of reason that dispelled the shadows of superstition. As Christianity embraced a more enlightened perspective, the witch hunts faded into history, leaving behind a cautionary tale of the dangers of irrationality.

The transition from the belief in witchcraft to a more rational worldview marked a crucial turning point in human history. As societies embraced scientific inquiry and enlightenment principles, the grip of superstition gradually loosened.

With the rise of scientific thought, phenomena once attributed to witchcraft were explained through empirical observation and experimentation. Natural laws replaced supernatural explanations, leading to a deeper understanding of the world around us.

Figures like Galileo Galilei and Johannes Kepler played pivotal roles in challenging entrenched beliefs and advancing scientific knowledge. Their contributions paved the way for a new era of exploration and discovery, where curiosity and evidence-based reasoning took precedence over superstition.

As the Enlightenment spread across Europe, attitudes towards witchcraft began to shift. Intellectuals and philosophers questioned traditional beliefs, advocating for tolerance, reason, and individual liberty. The ideals of the Enlightenment fostered a culture of critical thinking and skepticism, undermining the legitimacy of witch trials and persecutions.

The decline of witchcraft belief also coincided with broader social and political changes. The rise of secularism and the separation of church and state contributed to the waning influence of religious authorities in matters of law and governance. Legal reforms and human rights movements sought to protect individuals from unjust accusations and arbitrary persecution.

Today, the belief in witchcraft persists in some cultures, often intertwined with folklore, tradition, and spirituality. However, in most parts of the world, witchcraft is regarded as a relic of the past, a reminder of humanity's susceptibility to fear and ignorance.

In conclusion, the transition from witchcraft belief to a more rational worldview reflects the triumph of reason over superstition. It is a testament to the enduring power of human intellect and the capacity for enlightenment and progress.

The belief in witchcraft marked a significant chapter in human history, characterized by fear, superstition, and persecution. However, as societies progressed and embraced scientific inquiry, this belief gradually faded into obscurity. Here's how the story unfolds:

In ancient times, witchcraft was deeply ingrained in many cultures, often associated with supernatural powers and mysterious rituals. Individuals accused of practicing witchcraft were feared and ostracized, leading to widespread persecution and violence.

During the Middle Ages, Europe was gripped by a fervent belief in witchcraft, fueled by religious fervor and social upheaval. The Catholic Church played a central role in demonizing witches and conducting brutal witch hunts, resulting in the execution of thousands of innocent people.

The Renaissance period witnessed a shift towards humanism and rational thought, laying the groundwork for the eventual decline of witchcraft beliefs. Scholars and intellectuals began to question traditional superstitions, advocating for empirical observation and logical reasoning.

The Scientific Revolution of the 17th century further challenged supernatural explanations, as pioneers like Galileo Galilei and Isaac Newton revolutionized our understanding of the natural world. Their discoveries undermined the credibility of witchcraft accusations, as phenomena once attributed to magic could now be explained through scientific principles.

The Enlightenment of the 18th century ushered in an era of reason, tolerance, and secularism. Enlightenment thinkers rejected dogma and superstition, advocating for individual rights, freedom of thought, and the separation of church and state. Witchcraft trials became increasingly rare as societies embraced rationality and humanistic values.

Today, belief in witchcraft persists in some cultures, often as a cultural or spiritual practice rather than a genuine fear of malevolent witches. In many parts of the world, however, witchcraft is viewed as a relic of the past, a reminder of humanity's capacity for irrationality and injustice.

In conclusion, the decline of belief in witchcraft reflects the triumph of reason and enlightenment over superstition and fear. It is a testament to the enduring power of human intellect and the ongoing quest for knowledge and understanding.

Footnotes:

1. Check out the Fourteenth Annual Report of the Bureau of Ethnology, 1892-1893, page 150 for more information.

2. References to early Christian writings: Irenaeus, Justin Martyr, Epiphanius, and Eusebius. See their works for details.

3. The snake mentioned here resembles a stick but is flexible, not stiff.

4. "Octavius," a dialogue by M. Minucius Felix, can be found in Ante-Nicene Christian Library, Volume XIII, page 451 ff.

5. In "Octavius," Chapter 38, Socrates is humorously referred to as "scurra Atticus."

6. Images reproduced from the Fourteenth Annual Report of the Bureau of Ethnology, page 670.

7. Detailed information can be found in the Fourteenth Annual Report of the Bureau of Ethnology, Part 2, page 673 ff., and also in Drake's "Tecumseh."

8. More illustrations from the Fourteenth Annual Report of the Bureau of Ethnology, page 670.

9. Some Christian Apocrypha attribute miracles to Jesus himself, which would be considered criminal.

10. In 1521, a surgeon in Hamburg was executed for witchcraft for saving a baby's life that a midwife had given up on. See Soldan's "Hexenprocesse," page 326.

11. See, for example, the Fourteenth Annual Report of the Bureau of Ethnology, 1892-1893, page 561.

12. The Ghost Dance, taught to Native Americans by the prophet Wovoka, illustrates a deeply religious spirit. For more, see the Annual Report of the American Bureau of Ethnology, 1892-1893.

13. The term "black magic" originated from a corruption of the word "necromancy" into "nigromancy."

14. References from "De Vanitate Scientiarum" by Agrippa von Nettesheim. See "Hexenprocesse" by Soldan, page 325.

15. Images reproduced from the original edition of "Occulta Philosophia," Chapter XXVII.

16. "De Incertitudine et Vanitate Scientiarum et Artium, atque Excellentia Verbi Dei Declamatio," published in 1530.

17. Quotations from "Paciandi De Christianorum balneis." For more, see Smith-Cheetham Dictionary of Christian Antiquities, page 652.

18. References to "De vita et miraculis patrum Italicorum libri IV." See Roskoff's "Geschichte des Teufels," page 292.

19. Historical details can be found in Massmann's "Die deutschen Abschwörungs-, Glaubens-, Beicht- und Betformeln" and Roskoff's "Geschichte des Teufels," among others.

20. The original Old Low-German text reads as follows...

21. Information from "Illustrium miraculorum et historiarum memorabilium libri XII" by Cæsarius Heisterbacensis.

22. The original text is from fol. 2a column 1 of Codex miso (D) in the Royal Library at Düsseldorf.

23. For a summary, see Wolfgang Menzel's "Deutsche Literaturgeschichte," pages 310-312, and Roskoff's "Geschichte des Teufels," pages 317-326.

24. Quote from Cistercian monk Cæsarius of Heisterbach.

25. Additional reading on the topic can be found in Roskoff's work, pages 535-545.

26. Regarding the "Processus Sathanæ," see Dr. R. Stintzing's "Geschichte der populären Litteratur des röm. can. Rechts in Deutschland," and Roskoff's book, which includes extracts from Stintzing.

27. From Gustav Könnecke's "Bilderatlas zur Geschichte der deutschen Nationallitteratur," page 93.

28. Details from Floegel's "Geschichte des Grotesk-Komischen," edited by Fr. W. Ebeling.

29. For more, see Encyclopedia Britannica, Volume XX, page 258.

30. Information published by Georg Conrad Horst in "Zauberbibliothek," Volume I, page 92 ff.

31. Reference to Agrippa von Nettesheim's "De occulta philosophia," page 459.

32. From Gerhard's "Geomantic Astronomy," as cited in Agrippa von Nettesheim's "De occulta philosophia," liber III., chap. XI.

33. Petrus de Albano's week "exploration" method, as reproduced from "Elementa Magica" in Agrippa von Nettesheim's "De occulta philosophia," page 465.

34. Reference to Agrippa von Nettesheim's "De occulta philosophia," page 560.

35. Translated from Carus Sterne's "Die allgemeine Weltanschauung," page 56.

36. Translated by E. F. L. Gauss from "Deutscher Liederhort" (Erk & Böhme), Volume III.

37. Translation by E. F. L. Gauss, from "Das Kloster," Stuttgart, 1846, Volume II, Part I, page 176.

38. This poem is likely the one referred to by Schiller in a letter to Goethe dated May 23, 1797.

39. For a detailed exploration of this subject, see President Andrew Dickson White's two-volume work, "A History of the Warfare of Science with Theology in Christendom," New York, 1896.

14

THE INQUISITION

The Dark Era of Heretic Persecution

One of the darkest chapters in history unfolds in the persecution of those labeled as followers of the Devil: heretics, sectarians, and witches. Imagine being accused of obscene ceremonies and accused of worshipping the Devil, solely based on dissenting beliefs. This was the reality for groups like the Manichees, Montanists, Cathari, Albigenses, and others. During times when belief in witchcraft and Satan's power was widespread, no one was safe from accusations. Even those who resisted authority, like the Stedingers, faced brutal punishment after being branded as Devil-worshippers.

The persecution wasn't just limited to obscure groups. The Knights Templar, one of the wealthiest and most orthodox Christian orders, were accused of heinous idolatry, driven by a king's greed for their riches. Countless individuals, both poor and wealthy, fell victim to this superstition, often to serve the interests of the powerful or out of sheer ignorance.

The witch-hunt hysteria was a plague of the times, not solely the fault of the Church but certainly not absolved from it. Both Catholic and Protestant authorities not only upheld witch-hunting but actively enforced it, resulting in devastating consequences.

Heretics were lumped in with witches and wizards, seen as worshippers of Satan. Biblical verses were twisted to justify their persecution, with some leaders advocating death for those who dared to deviate from the established faith. Priscillian, a bishop of Spain, was among the first heretics to face torture and execution in 385 AD. His followers saw him as a martyr, despite the Church's condemnation.

Papal authority played a significant role in institutionalizing persecution. Popes like Innocent III and Gregory IX wielded immense power, using the Inquisition as a tool to crush dissent and maintain control. The establishment of the Dominican order, tasked with hunting heretics, marked a dark turn in Church history. These "sleuth-hounds of the Lord" enforced papal decrees with ruthless efficiency, solidifying the Church's dominance and perpetuating a reign of terror.

As papal authority solidified and the Inquisition gained momentum, heretic persecution reached horrifying heights. The Council of Toulouse in 1229 formalized the Inquisition's procedures, empowering the Church to prosecute heretics with unprecedented efficiency. Pope Gregory IX further cemented the Inquisition's role by establishing the Holy Office, a specialized tribunal dedicated to rooting out heresy.

Under this system, the Dominicans emerged as the enforcers of orthodoxy, tasked with ferreting out heretics and stamping out dissent. Their zealous pursuit earned them the ominous nickname "the sleuth-hounds of the Lord," as they relentlessly hunted down those deemed guilty of deviating from Catholic doctrine.

The Inquisition spread its reach far and wide, extending its influence across Europe and beyond. No corner was immune from its scrutiny, as bishops and secular authorities alike were compelled to assist in the identification and punishment of heretics. The threat of persecution loomed large, casting a shadow of fear over anyone who dared to question the Church's authority.

The impact of this era of persecution was profound, leaving a legacy of fear, mistrust, and trauma in its wake. Countless lives were destroyed, communities torn apart, and intellectual freedom stifled under the weight of religious orthodoxy. It was a dark period in history, one marked by fanaticism, intolerance, and the unchecked abuse of power in the name of faith.

In 1484, Pope Innocent VIII issued a bull called "Summis desiderantes affectibus," which gave a new boost to witch prosecutions. In Germany, two inquisitors, Heinrich Institoris (also known as Krämer) and Jacob Sprenger, had been facing resistance in carrying out their duties. The Pope backed them up, aiming to strengthen the Catholic faith and curb the perceived dangers of witchcraft.

While Innocent VIII's bull was directed at Germany, subsequent popes like Alexander VI, Julius II, Leo X, and

Hadrian IV issued similar bulls, urging inquisitors to root out witchcraft in the name of defending the faith.

This bull prompted the writing of the infamous "Malleus Maleficarum," or Witch-Hammer. Endorsed by the Pope and Emperor Maximilian, it served as a manual for prosecuting alleged witches. When Sprenger and Institoris presented it to the theological faculty of Cologne in 1487, they faced initial reluctance but eventually gained approval.

The Witch-Hammer became the go-to guide for zealots, shaping attitudes towards witchcraft for centuries. Its content is characterized by poor writing, irrational ideas, and villainous intentions. It advocated for brutal interrogation methods and offered twisted advice to inquisitors, such as assuming guilt if the accused denied belief in witchcraft.

Victims of the Inquisition had little recourse, as witchcraft was considered an exceptional crime exempt from standard legal procedures. Pope Boniface VIII's maxim "simply and squarely, without the noise and form of lawyers and judges" epitomized the approach taken.

Today, it's challenging to comprehend how such beliefs and practices were ever accepted in society, especially in an era marked by more rational thinking and rigorous investigation.

The Witch-Hammer, as endorsed by Pope Innocent VIII and Emperor Maximilian, wielded immense influence over witch trials and prosecutions. Its twisted logic and cruel recommendations guided inquisitors in their ruthless pursuit of alleged witches.

One of the most disturbing aspects of the Witch-Hammer was its insistence on obtaining confessions through torture.

Inquisitors were instructed to use brutal methods to extract information, regardless of the accused's guilt or innocence. The book even suggested that denial of witchcraft itself was a crime, sealing the fate of those who protested their innocence.

For those unfortunate enough to be caught in the Inquisition's grip, there was little hope for a fair trial. The Witch-Hammer advocated for a swift and merciless approach, with acquittals being rare occurrences. Instead, the accused were often handed over to secular authorities for execution, with burning at the stake being a common fate.

What's particularly chilling is the lack of support for the accused during these trials. The Inquisition operated outside the bounds of normal legal procedures, allowing for unchecked abuse and manipulation. Even confessions obtained under duress were considered valid, leading to countless innocent lives being destroyed.

Looking back, it's hard to fathom how such barbaric practices were ever justified in the name of justice or religion. The Witch-Hammer stands as a stark reminder of the dangers of fanaticism and unchecked power, serving as a cautionary tale for future generations.

Due to a strong religious conviction, as evidenced by the Malleus Maleficarum authored by John Trithemius, Abbot of the Monastery of Spongheim (1442-1516), who, at the behest of Joachim, Markgrave of Brandenburg, conducted extensive research on the subject, presenting his findings in a four-volume work completed on October 16, 1508, at the age of sixty-six.

Trithemius identified four categories of witches and

wizards: those causing harm through poison or natural means, those using magical formulas, those personally communicating with the Devil, and those who have made pacts with the Devil. He argued that the only way to protect society from their malevolent influence was by eradicating them, preferably through burning alive.

According to Trithemius, witches were widespread, with even the smallest village harboring at least one. However, he lamented the scarcity of judges willing to punish these crimes against God and nature. He highlighted the dire consequences of witchcraft, including illness and death among both humans and animals, often unnoticed by the afflicted.

In response to the perceived threat of witchcraft, extreme measures were employed, including the use of torture. Suspected individuals underwent fire and water ordeals, with the latter being favored. The water ordeal involved submerging the accused, with their innocence or guilt determined by their ability to float or sink.

The torture methods employed were barbaric and horrifying, including thumbscrews, tongs, racks, Spanish boots, and devices like the "Scavenger's Daughter" and "Iron Virgin." The ingenuity in creating these instruments of torment was matched only by the cruelty of their use.

An example of the brutality inflicted upon those accused of witchcraft is the case of a woman in 1631. She endured relentless torture over several hours, including burning, suspension, and physical mutilation, all in a relentless effort to extract a confession.

The story of Veit, a farmer falsely accused of witchcraft, illustrates the tragic consequences of superstition and hysteria.

Despite his innocence, Veit faced torture and eventual execution, with even scholars and theologians agreeing on his guilt.

The history of witch prosecutions is rife with countless similar tales of injustice and suffering, characterized by detailed yet absurd accusations. Each case serves as a poignant reminder of the dangers of unchecked fear and fanaticism.

The era marked by the Malleus Maleficarum, penned by John Trithemius, Abbot of the Monastery of Spongheim, stands as a chilling testament to the depths of superstition and fear that gripped society during the late Middle Ages and early Renaissance. Trithemius, at the request of Joachim, Markgrave of Brandenburg, delved into the obscure realm of witchcraft with meticulous fervor, culminating in a comprehensive four-volume work completed in 1508.

Within the pages of the Malleus Maleficarum, Trithemius meticulously classified witches and wizards into four distinct categories, each more menacing than the last. From those wielding poison and natural means to those communing directly with the Devil, Trithemius painted a grim picture of occult influence permeating every corner of society. His grim assessment concluded that the only recourse against such malevolent forces was their eradication, preferably through the fiery punishment of burning alive.

Yet, despite Trithemius's solemn warnings, the pervasive presence of witchcraft persisted, infesting even the most remote villages with its shadowy influence. The scarcity of judges willing to confront this diabolical threat left communities vulnerable to its insidious grasp. Trithemius mourned the apathy and ignorance that allowed witches to wreak havoc unchecked, their sinister deeds causing untold suffering among both humans and animals, often unbeknownst to their victims.

In response to the perceived epidemic of witchcraft, authorities resorted to increasingly extreme measures, including the widespread use of torture. Suspected individuals faced harrowing trials by fire and water, their innocence or guilt determined by archaic rituals that subjected them to unimaginable torment. The water ordeal, in particular, became a favored method of testing, with its roots tracing back through centuries of legal tradition and ecclesiastical decree.

The instruments of torture employed by inquisitors were as ingenious as they were barbaric, designed to extract confessions through unspeakable pain and suffering. From thumbscrews to racks, from Spanish boots to devices like the "Scavenger's Daughter" and the "Iron Virgin," each instrument served as a grim testament to humanity's capacity for cruelty.

One need only look to the tragic fate of Veit, the hapless farmer falsely accused of witchcraft, to understand the human toll exacted by this hysteria. Despite his innocence, Veit faced a relentless onslaught of torture and interrogation, culminating in a horrifying execution that served as a stark reminder of the injustices perpetrated in the name of superstition.

The history of witch prosecutions is a dark chapter in humanity's collective narrative, characterized by a potent blend of fear, fanaticism, and ignorance. Each tale of persecution serves as a poignant reminder of the dangers posed by unchecked hysteria and the profound consequences of succumbing to the darkness within.

As the power of the papacy solidified and the Inquisition gained momentum, the persecution of heretics reached terrifying heights. The Council of Toulouse in 1229 formalized the procedures of the Inquisition, granting the Church the authority to prosecute heretics with unprecedented efficiency. Pope Gregory IX further entrenched the role of the Inquisition by establishing the Holy Office, a specialized tribunal dedicated to rooting out heresy.

Within this framework, the Dominicans emerged as the enforcers of orthodoxy, charged with ferreting out heretics and extinguishing dissent. Their fervent pursuit earned them the chilling moniker "the sleuth-hounds of the Lord," reflecting their relentless quest to hunt down those deemed guilty of straying from Catholic doctrine.

The Inquisition extended its influence far and wide, casting its net across Europe and beyond. No corner was immune from its scrutiny, as bishops and secular authorities were compelled to aid in the identification and punishment of heretics. The specter of persecution loomed large, instilling fear in anyone who dared to challenge the authority of the Church.

The repercussions of this era of persecution were profound, leaving behind a legacy of fear, distrust, and trauma. Countless lives were shattered, communities torn asunder, and intellectual inquiry stifled under the weight of religious orthodoxy. It was a dark chapter in history, characterized by fanaticism, intolerance, and the unchecked abuse of power in the name of faith.

The persecution of heretics and dissenters during this period was not only fueled by religious fervor but also by political machinations and economic interests. The accusations of heresy often served as convenient pretexts for consolidating power, settling scores, or seizing wealth.

Innocent III, one of the most influential popes of the Middle Ages, wielded the authority of the papacy with unmatched vigor. He saw the suppression of heresy as a means of preserving the unity and dominance of the Catholic Church. His decrees and actions laid the groundwork for the systematic persecution of those deemed to be deviating from orthodox belief.

The establishment of the Inquisition as a formal institution marked a turning point in the history of religious intolerance. With its network of spies, informants, and inquisitors, the Church set out to eradicate any challenge to its dogma. The methods employed by the Inquisition were ruthless and relentless, including torture, imprisonment, and execution.

The role of the Dominicans in this dark chapter cannot be overstated. Tasked with rooting out heresy, they became the enforcers of orthodoxy, zealously carrying out the orders of the Church hierarchy. Their unwavering commitment to stamping out dissent earned them a fearsome reputation that reverberated throughout Europe.

The legacy of the Inquisition is one of fear, oppression, and suffering. Countless lives were lost, families torn apart, and communities decimated in the name of religious purity. The scars left by this era of persecution are still felt today, serving as a stark reminder of the dangers of unchecked zealotry and intolerance.

In Florence's Santa Maria Novella, there's a famous fresco by Simone Memmi called "Domini canes," which symbolizes the idea of the Inquisition. It depicts a pack of hounds driving away wolves from a sheepfold, representing the pursuit of heretics.

During the reign of Pope Gregory IX (1227-1241), Conrad of Marburg was dispatched to Germany with sweeping authority to summon anyone suspected of witchcraft before his tribunal. His mission? To bring those found guilty to the stake. Conrad, driven by fervent zeal, obeyed his orders with gusto, considering the Pope's word as divine. Despite facing resistance, even from powerful church figures, Conrad pressed on, sparing no one in his pursuit. His methods were brutal; false accusations were accepted, while legitimate defenses were denied. Innocent lives were lost to his fanaticism.

Even when confronted with opposition, Rome remained steadfast in its mission. Pope Urban V, in 1362, issued a bull titled "In cæna Domini," condemning heresy unequivocally and intensifying the crackdown on dissenters.

However, not everyone welcomed the Inquisition with open arms. In Germany, Conrad faced significant pushback, culminating in his assassination in 1233. Yet, rather than deterring the Inquisition, his martyrdom only solidified its presence.

In France, the Inquisition thrived, fueled by support from kings like Louis the Pious and Philip the Fair. In Spain, Torquemada and Ximenes were notorious for their relentless persecution of heretics, sparing no one, not even Archbishop Carranza.

The Inquisition's methods were horrific, with torture, coercion, and false confessions leading to countless executions. Even those who recanted faced punishment, as seen in the case of the Prior of St. Germain, forced to publicly renounce his beliefs.

Despite intermittent lulls, like during the reign of Charles VI in France, where witchcraft prosecutions decreased due to papal infighting, the Inquisition's grip remained firm. In the face of mounting opposition, its atrocities continued, leaving a trail of devastation in its wake.

As the Inquisition gained momentum, its reach extended across Europe, leaving a trail of fear and devastation in its wake. In France, the flames of persecution were fanned by figures like Hugo de Beniols, who oversaw the burning of numerous individuals accused of witchcraft, including the elderly Angèle, Lady of Labarthe, on ludicrous charges of consorting with Satan and bearing monstrous offspring.

Meanwhile, in Germany, opposition to the Inquisition mounted, with the German Diet in Mainz openly defying Conrad of Marburg's authority and passing a vote of censure against him. Conrad's relentless pursuit of heretics ultimately led to his demise, as noblemen intercepted and killed him near Marburg in 1233. Yet, his martyrdom only fueled the Inquisition's zeal.

In Spain, the Inquisition flourished under the likes of Torquemada and Ximenes, who showed no mercy in their pursuit of heretics. Even high-ranking church officials like Archbishop Carranza found themselves ensnared in its web of persecution.

The Inquisition's methods were nothing short of barbaric, with torture, coercion, and false confessions leading to count-less executions. The story of the Prior of St. Germain serves as a chilling reminder of the lengths to which the Inquisition would go to maintain its grip on power.

Despite sporadic resistance and temporary lulls in persecution, such as during the reign of Charles VI in France, where papal infighting briefly lessened the intensity of witchcraft prosecutions, the Inquisition's reign of terror remained largely unchecked. Its atrocities continued unabated, leaving a dark stain on European history.

As the Inquisition tightened its grip, its influence spread like wildfire across Europe, leaving a trail of fear and devastation in its wake. In France, figures like Hugo de Beniols oversaw the burning of numerous individuals accused of witchcraft, including elderly Angèle, Lady of Labarthe, on ludicrous charges of consorting with Satan and bearing monstrous offspring.

Meanwhile, in Germany, resistance to the Inquisition mounted. The German Diet in Mainz openly defied Conrad of Marburg's authority, passing a vote of censure against him. Conrad's relentless pursuit of heretics ultimately led to his demise when noblemen intercepted and killed him near Marburg in 1233. Yet, his martyrdom only fueled the Inquisition's zeal.

In Spain, the Inquisition thrived under figures like Torquemada and Ximenes, who showed no mercy in their pursuit of heretics. Even high-ranking church officials like Archbishop Carranza found themselves ensnared in its web of persecution.

The Inquisition's methods were barbaric, with torture, coercion, and false confessions leading to countless executions. The story of the Prior of St. Germain serves as a chilling reminder of the lengths to which the Inquisition would go to maintain its grip on power.

Despite sporadic resistance and temporary lulls in persecution, such as during the reign of Charles VI in France, where papal infighting briefly lessened the intensity of witchcraft prosecutions, the Inquisition's reign of terror remained largely unchecked. Its atrocities continued unabated, leaving a dark stain on European history.

In the 15th century, Johannes Nider, a Dominican monk from Germany, published a book titled "Witches and Their Deceptions," adding fuel to the fire of the Inquisition's fervor. At the same time, Pope Eugene IV encouraged inquisitors to act with swift and severe judgment, sparing no leniency for those accused of heresy.

One particularly chilling case involved William von Edelin, Prior of St. Germain, who publicly recanted his disbelief in witchcraft after preaching against it. Forced to confess to ludicrous crimes and blasphemies, Edelin's ordeal serves as a harrowing example of the Inquisition's grip on the minds and bodies of its victims.

In 1458, J. Nicolaus Jaquerius further fanned the flames with his publication, "The Heretics' Scourge," which highlighted Edelin's case as evidence of the reality of witchcraft. With opposition dwindling, the Inquisition's power remained unchecked, leading to more heinous acts of persecution.

One such instance occurred when Inquisitor Pierre le Broussart, acting in the absence of the Bishop of Arras, coerced individuals to falsely confess to crimes associated with the Waldenses. Despite promises of leniency, these individuals were ultimately burned at the stake, their pleas of innocence falling on deaf ears.

The relentless pursuit of heretics and the spread of fear and terror across Europe marked the height of the Inquisition's power, leaving behind a legacy of suffering and injustice that would endure for centuries.

In the 15th century, the Inquisition's grip tightened as Johannes Nider, a Dominican monk, penned "Witches and Their Deceptions," adding to the hysteria. Meanwhile, Pope Eugene IV urged inquisitors to act ruthlessly, prompting a wave of persecution.

A poignant case unfolded with William von Edelin, Prior of St. Germain, who renounced skepticism on witchcraft after preaching against it. Forced to confess to absurd crimes, his story epitomized the Inquisition's coercion tactics.

In 1458, J. Nicolaus Jaquerius's "The Heretics' Scourge" highlighted Edelin's case, solidifying fears of witchcraft. The Inquisition, with dwindling opposition, continued its brutal crusade.

Pierre le Broussart, acting as a de facto inquisitor, coerced false confessions from individuals accused of Waldensian ties. Despite assurances, they were burned alive, their cries of innocence ignored.

This relentless pursuit and climate of fear marked the Inquisition's apex, leaving a legacy of suffering and injustice that haunted Europe for centuries.

As the 15th century unfolded, the Inquisition's grip on Europe tightened further. A Dominican monk named Johannes Nider added fuel to the fire with his treatise "Witches and Their Deceptions," fueling hysteria and paranoia.

Meanwhile, Pope Eugene IV encouraged inquisitors to act with unyielding severity, giving them carte blanche to pursue suspected heretics without restraint. This directive only exacerbated the climate of fear and suspicion that permeated society.

One notable case that exemplifies the Inquisition's tactics was that of William von Edelin, the Prior of St. Germain. Initially skeptical of claims of witchcraft, Edelin was coerced into confessing to heinous crimes he did not commit after facing intense pressure from inquisitors.

The publication of "The Heretics' Scourge" by J. Nicolaus Jaquerius in 1458 further fueled fears of witchcraft and provided justification for the Inquisition's brutal methods. This period saw a marked increase in the persecution of alleged heretics, with the Inquisition showing no mercy to those accused.

One particularly egregious example of the Inquisition's cruelty was the case of Pierre le Broussart, who falsely accused individuals of ties to the Waldensian movement. Despite promises of leniency, these individuals were ultimately burned alive, their protests of innocence falling on deaf ears.

The relentless pursuit of suspected heretics and witches during this period left a dark stain on European history, with countless lives lost and communities torn apart by fear and suspicion.

The tale of Agnes Bernauer, often dubbed "The Angel of Augsburg," serves as a chilling reminder of the dark and unjust realities of witch prosecutions in the past. Agnes, a young woman of remarkable beauty born around 1410 in

Biberach, found herself entangled in a tragic love affair with Albrecht, Duke of Bavaria.

Despite her humble origins as the daughter of a barber and a mere servant girl in Augsburg, Agnes captured the heart of Duke Albrecht with her golden hair and noble countenance. Their love, though unconventional, blossomed, leading Albrecht to take her to his residence in County Vohnburg.

However, Duke Ernest, Albrecht's father, grew increasingly concerned about the lack of a legitimate heir to the duchy and pressured his son to marry the daughter of Duke Erik of Brunswick. Albrecht, steadfast in his love for Agnes, refused, prompting Duke Ernest to resort to drastic measures to separate them.

At a public tournament, Duke Ernest barred Albrecht from participating, citing neglect of his duties for the sake of a concubine. Enraged, Albrecht immediately recognized Agnes as his wife and bestowed upon her the title of Duchess Agnes. Despite this gesture, Agnes lived in constant fear of Duke Ernest's wrath, a fear that tragically proved justified.

In Albrecht's absence, Duke Ernest seized Agnes and falsely accused her of witchcraft, orchestrating a sham trial that condemned her to death by drowning in the river. Despite the efforts of onlookers moved by her plight, Agnes perished at the hands of the executioner, her innocence cruelly denied.

In the aftermath of Agnes's death, Albrecht vowed revenge against his father, igniting a bitter conflict that ultimately led to reconciliation through the intervention of the Emperor. Duke Ernest, plagued by guilt, erected a chapel over Agnes's grave and ordered masses to be held in her honor.

Agnes Bernauer's memory endured, immortalized in

poetry and cherished by the people of Bavaria as a symbol of innocence wronged. Yet, her tragic tale serves as a sobering reminder of the injustices perpetrated in the name of witch-craft, a legacy that continues to haunt humanity to this day.

Footnotes:

1. Check out Epistle 15 to Turribius for more details.

2. For further reading, see Roskoff's "History of the Devil," volumes 2, pages 215-216.

3. The images on pages 312-320 are reproduced from Picart.

4. For more information on Conrad von Marburg, see works by Henke (Marburg, 1861) and Beck (Breslau, 1861). Conrad was the confessor of Elizabeth, widow of the Land-grave of Thuringia, who underwent severe corporal punish-ment and was later sainted. It's astonishing but true that a book defending Conrad's actions as an inquisitor was pub-lished by Kaltner under the title "Konrad von Marburg und die Inquisition in Deutschland" (Prague, 1882).

5. Sources: Lamothe-Langon, volume 3, page 299, and Soldan, page 193.

6. Additional sources: F. Hoffmann's "History of the Inqui-sition" (Bonn, 1878), and Llorente's "History of the Spanish Inquisition," translated from Spanish.

7. For more on this topic, see Fr. Joannes Nider's "Suevi ordin. praedicat. s. theolog. profess. et hereticae pestis inquisi-toris, liber insignis de maleficiis et eorum deceptionibus."

8. Pope Eugene's circular letter to the Inquisitors of 1437

emphasized simplicity and straightforwardness in judgment, without the noise and formality of a trial.

9. See Raynald for the year 1451 for further information.

10. The book "Flagellum Haereticorum Fascinariorum" is often appended to the "Malleus Maleficarum."

11. Chapter 4 of the book contains the abjuration formula.

12. The Latin phrase "Simpliciter et de plano, absque advocatorum et judiciorum strepitu et figura" was commonly used by Pope Eugenius IV.

13. Check out Soldan's "Hexenprocesse," page 222, and Roskoff, volumes 1, pages 226-292, for more insights.

14. Giovanno Ballista Cibo, elected pope in 1484, was ironically nicknamed "Nocens" by the people due to his numerous illegitimate children. A humorous rhyme mocked him for his prolific offspring.

15. Refer to "Hexenprocesse," page 222, for additional details.

16. Damhouder's "Praxis rerum criminalium" underscored the authority of the Witch-Hammer as almost equal to the law.

17. The phrase "Simpliciter et de plano, absque advocatorum et judiciorum strepitu et figura" echoed Pope Eugenius IV's sentiments.

18. The Witch-Hammer advised the secular court to deliver verdicts without bloodshed, echoing the sentiment "ecclesia non sitit sanguinem" (the Church thirsts not for blood).

19. It should read "Soli Deo Gloria."

20. The author of the Witch-Hammer referred to the dungeon's filth as "carceris squalores."

21. This gruesome account is translated from König's "Ausgeburten des Menschenwahns," page 130. See also Soldan, pages 269-270, for more details.

22. Folk songs and various literary works have immortalized Agnes Bernauer's story. For a critical review of the legend and historical facts, check out Dr. Christian Meyer's article on Agnes Bernauer in "Die Gartenlaube," 1873, page 454.

15

THE AGE OF THE REFORMATION

The Reformation marked a significant shift in religious beliefs, but it didn't instantly erase the idea of the Devil. Instead, there was a growing tendency to view Satan through a psychological lens. Rather than seeing him as a literal being lurking in the world, people began to understand him as the embodiment of temptation found within ourselves—temptations like greed, pride, and the pursuit of worldly success.

As Christianity split into two camps—those loyal to Rome and those pushing for change in the Protestant movement—the Devil became a central figure in the debate. These turbulent times were ripe for satire and criticism, with both sides using the Devil as a rhetorical weapon.

Yet, amidst the turmoil, the moral seriousness of the reformers pushed the Church to address its own shortcomings.

Reformation wasn't confined to Protestant circles; it also prompted changes within the Roman Catholic Church itself. On the flip side, the counter-reformation, led by groups like the Jesuits, was driven by religious fervor but tainted by mystical beliefs and a lack of openness to progress and truth-seeking that characterized Protestantism.

This period saw a clash between Calvinism and Catholicism, depicted in satirical artworks like "Calvinism Tearing Down the Roman Empire," showing the tension between the two ideologies.

Overall, the Reformation era was marked by a complex interplay of religious fervor, political upheaval, and social change. While it brought about significant shifts in religious thought and practice, it also highlighted the enduring power of superstition and the struggle for truth and freedom.

During the Reformation era, there was a significant shift in how people perceived Satan and temptation. Instead of viewing Satan as a literal figure, many began to see him as a symbol of sin and temptation, reflecting internal struggles rather than external threats.

Martin Luther, a prominent figure of this time, was deeply influenced by these changing views. He saw the Devil as a powerful force constantly at odds with humanity, but he also believed in the triumph of God's truth over evil. Luther famously expressed his defiance against Satan, declaring that even if the world were filled with devils, God's truth would prevail.

Luther's belief in the Devil was both realistic and sincere. He often spoke of encountering the Devil in his daily life, even throwing his inkstand at him during moments of frustration.

Despite his fearlessness, Luther recognized the Devil's potency and warned against underestimating his influence.

Although Luther accepted some superstitions surrounding witchcraft and demonic possession, he approached such cases with caution, emphasizing the need for thorough investigation to avoid wrongful accusations.

Ultimately, Luther's teachings emphasized personal faith and moral responsibility over religious rituals and ceremonies. He believed that true salvation came from overcoming temptation on an individual level, rather than relying solely on external practices. For Luther, the struggle against temptation was a deeply personal journey, one that required inner strength and conviction rather than outward rituals or symbols.

Even though Martin Luther opposed persecutions, his beliefs indirectly contributed to the witch hunts that plagued both Catholic and Protestant countries during the Reformation.

One notable piece of Protestant literature from this period is Sigmund Feyerabend's Theatrum Diabolorum, a comprehensive collection of writings by Luther's followers exploring the existence, power, and behavior of demons. Although Luther's view of the Devil was simplistic, his emphasis on personal moral responsibility was commendable. He believed that individuals should actively resist evil without relying solely on religious rituals or institutions.

Feyerabend's work, while extensive, reflects the crude beliefs of Luther's followers, who attributed various vices and misfortunes to specific types of demons. Despite its lack of literary or theological sophistication, this body of literature reflects a rationalistic tendency to interpret evil as a reflection of human vice rather than external supernatural forces.

Over time, Protestant theologians began to view Satan as a symbolic representation of evil rather than a literal entity. This gradual shift mirrored broader cultural advancements in Protestant societies. Shakespeare's depiction of witches and demons, for example, demonstrates a more nuanced understanding of temptation and psychological complexity.

In Shakespeare's works, the Devil often symbolizes temptation or the darker aspects of human nature. This interpretation aligns with the idea that evil can take on many forms, including the seductive allure of alcohol or the deceptive appearance of piety.

This evolution in the portrayal of evil reflects a broader cultural shift towards a more nuanced understanding of human behavior and morality. While earlier depictions of the Devil were often crude and literal, as seen in the writings of Luther's followers, later works like Shakespeare's demonstrate a deeper exploration of the complexities of human nature.

In Shakespeare's plays, characters grapple with inner conflicts and moral dilemmas, often personified by the presence of supernatural beings like witches or demons. These figures represent not only external threats but also internal struggles, reflecting the psychological dimension of evil.

For instance, in "Macbeth," the witches symbolize the lure of ambition and the consequences of unchecked desire. Macbeth's consultation with the witches triggers a chain of events that ultimately leads to his downfall, highlighting the destructive power of greed and ambition.

Similarly, in "Hamlet," characters confront their own moral ambiguity and the blurred lines between good and evil. The line "The Devil hath power to assume a pleasing shape" underscores the idea that evil can disguise itself in appealing forms, deceiving even the most virtuous individuals.

Overall, Shakespeare's nuanced portrayal of evil challenges simplistic notions of morality and encourages audiences to examine the complexities of human behavior. This more sophisticated understanding of evil marks a departure from earlier theological interpretations and reflects the growing intellectual and cultural trends of the Renaissance period.

Milton's portrayal of the Devil in his epic poem "Paradise Lost" marked a significant departure from earlier depictions. In Milton's hands, Satan emerges as a complex and even sympathetic character, far removed from the crude caricatures of the past.

Milton's Devil possesses a sense of nobility, moral strength, and independence rarely seen in previous representations. Unlike the horned enchanters and mischievous imps of medieval lore, Milton's Satan is a figure of grandeur and dignity. Taine, a literary critic, aptly captures Milton's characterization, highlighting Satan's pride and self-respect, as well as his unwavering commitment to his own principles.

In "Paradise Lost," Satan's rebellion against the divine order is framed as a struggle for liberty and independence. His refusal to submit to what he perceives as unjust authority resonates with themes of defiance and resistance, reflecting the spirit of the English Revolution in which Milton himself was deeply involved.

Satan's appearance and demeanor in Milton's work exude

strength and stature. He is described as standing proudly, like a tower among his peers, a symbol of defiance and resolve. Despite his eventual defeat and torment, Satan embraces his fate with a sense of honor and glory, choosing suffering independence over servile happiness.

This transformation of the Devil from a mere adversary to a noble and even heroic figure reflects broader cultural shifts during Milton's time. As the traditional God-conception became associated with conservatism and stagnation, Satan came to embody the aspirations for progress and freedom.

While Milton's portrayal of Satan may seem radical compared to earlier depictions, it ultimately serves as a powerful exploration of the complexities of human nature and the eternal struggle between authority and autonomy.

However, the evolution of Satan's character in literature did not stop with Milton. As society progressed and ideologies shifted, so too did the depiction of the Devil.

In Milton's Satan, we see the seeds of a more nuanced understanding of rebellion and resistance against oppressive authority. This portrayal laid the groundwork for future interpretations that would challenge traditional notions of good and evil.

In the centuries following Milton, the Devil continued to undergo transformations in literature and culture. With the rise of Enlightenment thinking and the questioning of established beliefs, the Devil came to represent not only defiance but also skepticism and intellectual inquiry.

During the Romantic era, writers like Lord Byron and William Blake further explored the complexities of the human psyche through their depictions of the Devil. In their works, Satan became a symbol of individualism, passion, and the pursuit of knowledge.

In more recent times, the Devil has been reimagined in various forms, from the charming and seductive Lucifer in Neil Gaiman's "Sandman" series to the tormented and sympathetic Lucifer Morningstar in the television show "Lucifer." These portrayals reflect contemporary society's fascination with moral ambiguity and the blurred lines between good and evil.

Overall, the evolution of the Devil in literature reflects humanity's ongoing quest to understand the nature of evil, free will, and the human condition. As long as these questions remain unanswered, the Devil will continue to captivate our imaginations and challenge our perceptions of morality and truth.

In Protestant communities, folks didn't envision Satan as the epic figure from "Paradise Lost." Instead, they saw him through the lens of the New Testament, taking him as seriously as folks did in early Christian times. But unlike their predecessors, they were influenced by both the Reformation's moral seriousness and its focus on personal experience.

The middle class, in particular, wasn't into old-school practices like exorcisms or witch hunts. They were more concerned with saving their own souls. Two standout literary works from this period are "Pilgrim's Progress" and "The Heart of Man." Both dive deep into the inner workings of the human mind, offering valuable insights into self-reflection and analysis.

While we know the author of "Pilgrim's Progress," "The Heart of Man" was published anonymously. It first appeared in French, then German. It features illustrations depicting the human heart as a battleground between good and evil.

The journey begins with the heart in its natural state of waywardness. But as the sinner repents, the Holy Ghost takes over. The heart then becomes a sanctuary for divine influence, until worldly temptations and trials chip away at its resolve. Eventually, Satan and his crew make a comeback, leaving the heart in a worse state than before.

The illustrations culminate in depictions of the pious and the impious meeting their respective fates in the afterlife. The pious are welcomed into eternal bliss, while the impious face damnation in Hell.

What's intriguing about these illustrations is how they depict the soul's elements as external forces that enter, leave, and return. The heart itself is portrayed as a blank slate, its character shaped by the influences it harbors. This approach to understanding the soul aligns closely with modern psychological concepts, suggesting that the author was onto something deeper than he may have realized.

These illustrations offer a unique perspective on the human psyche, portraying its inner workings as a dynamic interplay of various forces. The images depict the heart not as a static entity, but as a vessel constantly influenced by external and internal factors.

In this interpretation, the self is not a fixed identity but rather a culmination of the elements that inhabit it. The illustrations suggest that our moral character and spiritual destiny are shaped by the interactions between these elements within our souls.

While the author's psychological framework may not

have been explicitly articulated, the drawings hint at a sophisticated understanding of human nature. They resonate with modern ideas about the complexity of the mind and the role of external influences in shaping our thoughts, feelings, and actions.

Overall, these illustrations offer a thought-provoking exploration of the human condition, inviting us to reflect on the forces that shape our moral and spiritual lives. They remind us that our journey towards self-discovery and redemption is a dynamic and ongoing process, influenced by both internal reflections and external challenges.

During the Reformation era, the persecution of witches took a temporary pause, only to be replaced by another dark obsession: the persecution of heretics. Both Catholic and Protestant authorities were guilty of tormenting dissenters, confiscating property, and even resorting to executions to enforce religious conformity. While Luther himself did not engage in persecution, others like Calvin and King Henry VIII were not so merciful.

Although the fear of witchcraft momentarily subsided, the belief in Satan's power lingered beneath the surface. This superstition persisted, leading to sporadic outbreaks of witch hysteria, even in Protestant territories. Influential figures like Calvin and King James I perpetuated these fears with their writings, while others fiercely defended the witch hunts with elaborate arguments and gruesome executions.

Despite some sensible voices, like Bishop Miron and Cardinal De Gondi in France, who approached cases of supposed demonic possession with skepticism and rational inquiry, the persecution of witches continued. In notorious cases like that of Urban Grandier, accusations of witchcraft often served as a pretext for personal vendettas and political agendas.

Protestant America was not immune to the witch hysteria. In Salem, Massachusetts, the infamous witch trials orchestrated by religious leaders like Increase and Cotton Mather led to mass hysteria, false accusations, and tragic executions. Even innocent individuals like Mr. Burroughs fell victim to the frenzy, highlighting the dangerous consequences of superstition and religious fanaticism.

While modern audiences may find these beliefs absurd, they were deeply entrenched in the religious worldview of the time. The abandonment of witchcraft as a credible threat marked a shift towards a more rational understanding of the natural world and a more enlightened approach to religion, paving the way for a more enlightened faith based on reason and justice rather than fear and superstition.

As societies progressed and Enlightenment ideals spread, the horrors of witch trials began to fade into history. Rationalism and scientific inquiry replaced superstition and fear, leading to a more enlightened understanding of the world. The notion of witches and demons manipulating reality gave way to a more nuanced appreciation of human psychology and natural phenomena.

The legacy of the witch trials served as a cautionary tale, reminding future generations of the dangers of unchecked religious fervor and the consequences of scapegoating marginalized groups. Scholars and thinkers dissected these events, analyzing the social, political, and psychological factors that contributed to the hysteria.

In the wake of these trials, societies grappled with

questions of justice, accountability, and religious tolerance. Legal systems evolved to protect the rights of the accused, while intellectual movements advocated for freedom of thought and expression. The witch trials became a symbol of the dangers of dogma and intolerance, inspiring movements for social reform and individual liberty.

Today, we look back on the era of witch trials with a mixture of horror and fascination, recognizing the importance of learning from the mistakes of the past. The stories of those who suffered unjustly serve as a reminder of the fragility of human rights and the enduring struggle for justice and equality.

As societies continued to advance, the legacy of the witch trials persisted in cultural memory, influencing literature, art, and popular culture. Writers and artists drew inspiration from these dark chapters of history, using them as allegories for contemporary issues such as prejudice, injustice, and abuse of power.

In literature, authors like Nathaniel Hawthorne, Arthur Miller, and Maryse Condé explored themes of scapegoating, paranoia, and mass hysteria in works like "The Scarlet Letter," "The Crucible," and "I, Tituba, Black Witch of Salem." These novels shed light on the psychological and social dynamics at play during witch trials, inviting readers to reflect on the dangers of mob mentality and the importance of individual conscience.

Similarly, in visual arts, painters and filmmakers depicted scenes of witch trials, capturing the chaos, fear, and injustice of these events. Works like Francisco Goya's "The Witches' Sabbath" and Dario Argento's film "Suspiria" reimagined the

witch trials through a modern lens, highlighting their enduring relevance and impact on contemporary culture.

As society became more secular and skeptical, the belief in
witchcraft waned, replaced by a more rational and scientific
worldview. Yet, the fascination with witches and the supernatural persisted, evolving into new forms of expression in
literature, film, and popular culture. From the bewitching
allure of characters like Hermione Granger in the "Harry
Potter" series to the eerie atmosphere of TV shows like
"American Horror Story: Coven," the archetype of the witch
continued to captivate audiences around the world.

In conclusion, while the era of witch trials may belong
to the past, its legacy endures in the collective consciousness
of humanity. By studying and reflecting on these historical
events, we gain insight into the complexities of human nature, the dangers of intolerance, and the enduring quest for
truth and justice in society.

Footnotes:

1. The *Hortus Deliciarum*, created in the late 12th
century, aimed to guide monks but also depicted temptations
leading them astray: the allure of city life and luxury, the
worldly power of abbots, money, laziness, and the joys of
gardening.

2. The illustration of the Empire, inscribed with "The gates
of hell shall not prevail against it," depicts German Protestant
princes among devils. It symbolizes Count Palatine Frederick
V's fall after losing the crown of Bohemia. The Prince Elector
of Saxony and the city of Venice, depicted, represent refusal

to join Calvinists. This image aimed to simplify scripture for common understanding.

3. Luther's purported inkstand incident, though doubted, aligns with his attitude towards Satan, as evidenced by numerous sources.

4. The authenticity of the letter requesting caution against deceit in witch trials is debated, yet reflects the skepticism prevalent during the time.

5. Image source: Könnecke, based on contemporary illustrations.

6. Notable works discussing witchcraft include: *De Lamiis et Strigibus* (1577), *De Magorum Daemonomania* (1579), *Tractatus de Confessionibus Maleficorum et Sagarum* (1589), *Daemonolatria* (1593), *Daemonologie* (1597), and *Disquisitiones Magicae* (1599).

7. The hymn "Nun Bitten Wir den Heiligen Geist" was believed to protect against witchcraft. It was sung by a superintendent to repel tormentors disguised as devils.

8. For further reading: *The Wonders of the Invisible World* by Cotton Mather and "New Chapters in the Warfare of Science" by Andrew Dickson White.

16

THE ABOLITION OF WITCH-PROSECUTION

Molitor and Erasmus.

The dark ages weren't just a time of questionable fashion choices and questionable hygiene—they were also plagued by some seriously messed-up beliefs about evil. Picture it: the Inquisition, witch trials, all that scary stuff straight out of your worst nightmares. But fear not, because eventually, humanity woke up from that fever dream, thanks to a little thing called science. As science started shining its light, those creepy shadows of superstition began to scatter, revealing just how bonkers those old beliefs really were.

Now, rewind to the late 1400s. You've got these two inquisitors, Sprenger and Institutoris, doing their evil thing with the Pope's blessing, while Dr. Ulrich Molitoris, a Constance attorney, decides enough is enough. He writes this pamphlet called "Dialogus de lamiis et pythonibus mulieribus," basically calling out the Inquisition for their shady practices. But even with other legal bigwigs like Alciatus and Ponzinibius backing him up, the powers that be weren't having it. They dismissed Molitoris's arguments, saying lawyers just didn't get the whole witchcraft deal.

Meanwhile, the world was still obsessed with all things spooky. Crazy stories, like Grünbeck's "New Interpretation of Strange Miracles" from 1507, were considered legit divine stuff. The weirder the tale, the more people bought into it. Case in point: in 1498, the hangman of Vienna straight-up refused to do his job on execution day. They had to scramble to find someone else to do the dirty work. And in 1576, Katharine Hensel nearly got the axe—literally—but her plea of innocence was so convincing, even the hangman couldn't go through with it. The trial got reversed, and the town ended up footing the bill for the whole mess.

Enter Erasmus of Rotterdam, dropping truth bombs in a letter from 1500, calling devil-contracts a load of bull. But guess what? Even his epic clapback couldn't stop the witch-burning bonanza sweeping across Europe.

Weier, Meyfart, and Loos.

A pivotal moment in history, albeit temporary and with restricted impact, occurred with the endeavor to halt the persecution of individuals accused of witchcraft. This initiative was spearheaded by Johannes Weier, a Protestant physician whose scholarly pursuits and worldly travels imbued him with a unique perspective. Born in Grave in 1515, Weier's academic journey led him to Paris and later to Africa, where he gained insights into sorcery. Following his sojourn in Crete, he assumed the esteemed role of body-physician to Duke William of Cleves. In 1563, Weier published a comprehensive work titled "De prætigiis Dæmonum et incantationibus ac Veneficiis," comprising six volumes. While he acknowledged the existence of supernatural entities and magical practices, he vehemently rejected the notion of witchcraft and pacts with demonic forces. Courageously, he indicted members of the clergy, accusing them of serving malevolent interests under the guise of religious duty. Inspired by Weier's convictions, notable figures such as William, Duke of Cleves, Frederic, Count of Palatine, and the Count of Niurwenar took decisive action to quell witch-hunting activities.

Two decades subsequent to Weier's endeavors, another luminary emerged in the form of Meyfart, a Protestant scholar and rector of the Latin school of Coburg. Meyfart's impassioned sermon, "Admonitions to the powerful princes and the conscientious preachers," served as a poignant rebuke directed at the Dominican fathers, who wielded authority as official witch prosecutors. He admonished them, invoking the specter of divine judgment, wherein they would be held accountable for the anguish inflicted upon their purported victims.

Despite the profound impact of Weier and Meyfart's interventions, a reactionary wave ensued. The enduring influence of witchcraft beliefs is evidenced by the issuance of a criminal ordinance in the Protestant Electorate of Saxony in 1572, threatening severe punishment, including death by immolation, for individuals suspected of consorting with malevolent entities.

In a tragic turn of events, Cornelius Loos, a respected canonicus and professor at the University of Treves, found himself at odds with prevailing orthodoxy. His discerning intellect led him to challenge the integrity of judges involved in witchcraft trials. Loos authored a seminal work, "De vera et falsa magia," which unfortunately never saw the light of day. Suppressed by authorities and incarcerated, Loos was compelled to recant publicly before ecclesiastical dignitaries in 1593. His demise in 1595, attributed to the plague, spared him from the prospect of execution by immolation. Recent rediscovery of Loos's manuscript, thanks to the efforts of Prof. George Lincoln Burr of Cornell University, sheds new light on his valiant efforts to oppose the prevailing superstitions of his time.

Three Distinguished Jesuits

Adam Tanner (1572-1632) and Paul Laymann (1575-1635), esteemed members of the Society of Jesus hailing from South Germany, offered sagacious counsel to judges embroiled in witchcraft trials. Their admonitions emphasized the imperative of exercising judiciousness and caution in such legal proceedings. Tragically, Tanner's demise during a journey in the hamlet of Unken led to an unusual controversy regarding his burial. Local parishioners, upon discovering a peculiar "hairy little imp" among his possessions, initially hesitated to accord him a Christian burial. This object, however, was later identified as an insect specimen intended for microscopic examination. The intervention of the Unken curate eventually assuaged concerns, allowing Tanner to be interred in the parish cemetery.

Equally noteworthy is the narrative of Friedrich Spee von Langenfeld (1591-1635), a revered Jesuit scholar and poet renowned for his steadfast opposition to the prevailing superstitions surrounding witch hunts. Spee's seminal work, "Cautio criminalis," published anonymously in 1631, served as a poignant appeal to German authorities to reassess their legal approach to witchcraft trials. As a pastor in Franconia, Spee personally witnessed the tragic fate of numerous individuals accused of witchcraft, an experience that deeply affected him. When questioned by Philip of Schoenborn, Bishop of Würzburg, about the premature greying of his hair, Spee attributed it to the anguish stemming from the unjust condemnation of countless innocents. Spee's candid confession to the Bishop regarding his authorship of "Cautio criminalis" underscored his unwavering commitment to rectifying the injustices perpetuated in the name of witchcraft prosecution.

In "Cautio criminalis," Spee denounced the lack of legal representation and defense afforded to accused individuals, denoting it as a fundamental violation of due process. He solemnly affirmed that none of the individuals he accompanied to the stake could be deemed legitimately convicted, echoing the sentiments of other pastors who shared similar experiences. Despite his steadfast adherence to Church doctrine, Spee vociferously protested against the flagrant abuses inherent in witchcraft trials, advocating instead for a more merciful approach.

Philip of Schoenborn's subsequent elevation to the position of Archbishop of Mainz was notable for the absence of witch burnings under his auspices, a testament to his conscientious leadership and commitment to justice.

Abatement of Witch-Prosecution.

Horst, in his Zauberbibliothek, Vi., 310, records a curious example of seventeenth-century fanaticism. An anonymous publication titled Druten-Zeitung, dating back to 1627, extolled the achievements of the Inquisition in crude verses. According to Horst, the author, a Protestant, expressed gratitude to God for the vigorous pursuit of witch eradication in neighboring Catholic territories. This underscores the persistence of witchcraft beliefs despite efforts by figures like Weier and Spee to challenge them. Nonetheless, a shift was evident as authorities began to doubt the necessity of witch prosecutions, prompting advocates of the cause to resort to anonymous publications.

Witch prosecutions were officially abolished in Holland in 1610 and in Geneva, Switzerland, in 1632.

Upon her accession to the throne, Queen Christina of Sweden issued a proclamation on February 16, 1649, extending to all Swedish territories in Germany, halting all witch prosecution activities. Meanwhile, Gabriel Naudé, a Frenchman who opposed witch prosecution, faced resistance from the Parliament of France, which upheld the belief in witchcraft and advocated for capital punishment. Nevertheless, Louis XIV decreed in 1672 that all witchcraft cases be dismissed, though he reintroduced the law for capital punishment of witches in 1683, albeit with restrictions on judicial authority.

In seventeenth-century England, Matthias Hopkins, known as the "witchfinder general," capitalized on the turmoil of the English civil wars to hunt witches. However, his methods eventually led to his downfall when they were applied to him, resulting in his demise in 1647. Witch prosecutions were officially abolished in England in 1682. Figures like Glanville and Dr. Webster engaged in debates over witchcraft beliefs, with the latter opposing Glanville's superstitious propositions. The English government intervened to halt Glanville's witch hunts, exemplifying a growing skepticism toward witchcraft.

Towards the end of the seventeenth century, dissent against belief in the Devil became increasingly vocal. Anton van Dale, a Dutch physician, challenged the attribution of pagan oracles to the Devil, instead attributing them to priestly fraud. His works laid the groundwork for reformers like Bekker and Thomasius, who openly denounced witchcraft as superstition, ultimately leading to the cessation of official witch prosecutions by state and church authorities.

Balthasar Bekker, a Dutch clergyman, authored "The Enchanted World" (De betoverde Weereld) from 1691 to 1693, critically examining beliefs in devils, witches, and legal proceedings against them. Despite facing opposition and condemnation, Bekker's work gained widespread popularity, contributing to a shift in public opinion. Christian Thomasius, a professor at the University of Halle, continued Bekker's legacy by staunchly opposing witch prosecution. His influential writings and condemnation of the practice played a pivotal role in ending official witch prosecutions and dispelling widespread fear of the Devil.

The Last Traces

The Inquisition persisted into the early nineteenth century in Spain, a nation deeply entrenched in its adherence to Roman Catholicism. In 1808, following the battle of Ramosiera, French forces led by General La Salle seized control of Toledo, uncovering the dungeons of the Inquisition. These subterranean cells were grim, cramped spaces, barely allowing a person to stand upright, and most prisoners emerged stiff and crippled from the mistreatment they endured. Unfortunately, both the prisoners and their liberators, a detachment of lancers, were besieged by an enraged Spanish mob, isolating them from the main French army. Despite General La Salle's efforts to intervene, he arrived too late, finding only the mutilated corpses of the slain.

In a hidden vault, General La Salle discovered a wooden statue of the Virgin Mary adorned in silk garments, with a golden halo encircling her head and holding the standard of the Inquisition in her right hand. While outwardly fair, her breast was encased in spiked armor, and her arms and hands were mechanized, concealed behind the statue. Inquisitorial servants explained to General La Salle that this statue was employed to extract confessions from heretics. Upon receiving the sacrament at the altar in the statue's dimly lit presence, the delinquent would be urged to confess again. Subsequently, two priests would lead the individual to a statue of the Sorrowful Mother, whose outstretched arms seemed to beckon the sinner into her embrace. However, as the arms closed, they would trap and impale the victim on spikes and knives.

Napoleon I officially disbanded the Inquisition in Spain on December 4, 1808, and a year later in Rome. Nevertheless, Ferdinand VII of Spain revived the Inquisition on June 21, 1813, with its final victims being a Jew burned at the stake and a Quaker schoolmaster hanged in 1826.

Descriptions of Hell

Father Caussin, Jesuit confessor to King Louis XIII, provided a vivid portrayal of hell in his work "La Cour Sainte," which gained considerable renown in his era. He likened hell to a deep, foul pit where all the refuse of the world congregates, a sentiment echoed by other theologians who described it as an abyss of despair devoid of hope. Similarly, the biblical depiction in the Book of Revelation portrays hell as an eternal furnace of fire, shrouded in darkness, inhabited by serpents and vipers, and characterized by ceaseless torment and anguish.

Justus Georg Schottel, a scholar of Brunswick-Lüneburg, delved into the intricacies of hellish tortures, envisioning a colossal iron wheel perpetually inflicting excruciating agony. His elaborate description conjures images of eternal suffering in burning pitch, searing sulfur, and red-hot iron, with the perpetual rotation of the wheel symbolizing never-ending torment. Schottel's depiction bears resemblance to the Buddhist Wheel of Life, underscoring the universality of the concept of eternal punishment across cultures.

Abraham a Sancta-Clara, a prominent preacher in Vienna in the early eighteenth century, expounded on the horrors of hell in his sermons, emphasizing the unfathomable misery awaiting sinners. Despite the intellectual awakening of the eighteenth century, beliefs in hell persisted, with theologians like Rev. Father Gilbert Baur describing hell as an infernal abyss where every nerve and artery is consumed by unrelenting fire, yet offering no respite from eternal suffering.

Slavonic folk songs further illustrate the indescribable torments of hell, depicting it as a place of ceaseless anguish where sinners are subjected to unimaginable pain and anguish for eternity. The vivid imagery of these songs, coupled with the grim descriptions of theologians, underscores the pervasive fear of damnation prevalent in both Europe and America.

Ultimately, the enduring belief in hell and its terrors reflects the profound influence of religious teachings on the human psyche, with descriptions of hell serving as cautionary tales intended to deter individuals from sin. Yet, amidst the terror of eternal damnation, there also arises a sense of resignation and defiance, as evidenced by the infidel farmer who stoically accepts his fate, refusing to succumb to the despair of hellish torment.

This resilience in the face of theological terror raises intriguing questions about the nature of faith, morality, and human resilience. The juxtaposition of religious descriptions of hell with the pragmatic acceptance of fate by non-believers highlights the complex interplay between religious indoctrination and personal conviction.

Furthermore, the persistence of beliefs in hell across

different cultures and historical periods underscores the enduring power of religious narratives to shape human thought and behavior. Despite advances in science, philosophy, and rational inquiry, the fear of divine punishment continues to exert a profound influence on individuals' lives, shaping their moral choices and ethical beliefs.

In modern times, the concept of hell has been subject to reinterpretation and critique, with some religious scholars advocating for a more metaphorical understanding of hell as a state of spiritual separation from the divine rather than a physical place of torment. Others have rejected the notion of hell altogether, viewing it as a relic of antiquated religious beliefs incompatible with contemporary values of compassion and justice.

Nevertheless, the imagery of hell continues to captivate the human imagination, serving as a potent symbol of the consequences of moral transgression and spiritual estrangement. Whether embraced as a literal truth or dismissed as a metaphorical construct, the concept of hell remains a central motif in religious discourse, inviting reflection on the nature of evil, suffering, and redemption in the human experience.

Schwenter and Kircher

The Jesuit order, known for its staunch adherence to Roman Catholic principles and strict obedience to ecclesiastical authority, was established with the explicit aim of combating Protestantism and promoting the Catholic Counter-Reformation. Consequently, among Protestants, it is often regarded as the most objectionable Catholic order.

However, notwithstanding criticism directed at the Jesuits, their methodologies, and doctrinal rigidity, it is undeniable that some of their members have achieved prominence as scholars. Athanasius Kircher stands out as one of the most distinguished scientists produced by the Jesuit order.

Born in Geisa, near Fulda, Germany, in 1601, Kircher held positions as a professor of philosophy and mathematics at the University of Würzburg before relocating to Avignon, France, during the tumultuous period of the Thirty Years' War. His travels included a journey to Malta accompanying Cardinal Frederick of Saxony, culminating in his appointment as a professor of mathematics and Hebrew in Rome. While Kircher's investigations may not have directly pertained to witchcraft prosecutions, they nonetheless contributed indirectly to the understanding of psychical phenomena.

One notable experiment associated with Kircher involved hens and pigeons, which perplexed psychologists of his time and continues to intrigue researchers today. Kircher's experiment, wherein he traced a line along a hen's bill with chalk, resulting in the hen remaining motionless in a seemingly paralyzed state until released by the experimenter's hand movements, gained widespread attention. However, it is worth noting that Kircher's attribution as the inventor of this experiment is disputed by some scholars.

Daniel Schwenter, who published his discovery a decade prior to Kircher's Ars Magna Lucis et Umbræ, is credited with originating the experiment. Despite this, Kircher's prominence ensured greater visibility for the phenomenon. This experiment, initially interpreted by Kircher as a manifestation of the hen's imagination, later became associated with magnetism, mesmerism, and eventually hypnotism in subsequent centuries. While the scientific significance of this phenomenon remains a subject of debate, its discovery marked a milestone in the scientific examination of psychical phenomena, contributing to a deeper understanding of abnormal states of consciousness.

Diabolism Developing into Pathology

In the mid-eighteenth century, Father John Joseph Gassner, vicar of Klösterle in Chur, a Roman Catholic clergyman, espoused the theory that the majority of diseases stemmed from demonic possession. Employing exorcism, Gassner purportedly cured both himself and his parishioners, garnering considerable attention and controversy. Mesmer, at the behest of the Elector of Bavaria, investigated Gassner's purported miracles, attributing them to spiritualistic magnetic influences, while Lavater attributed the curative effects solely to the name of Jesus.

Gassner's exorcisms sparked renewed interest in the question of the Devil's existence, prompting widespread discourse and debate. Various publications, including a pamphlet anonymously authored by Professor Köster of Giessen, articulated orthodox perspectives on the Devil's existence, contrasting with rationalistic interpretations presented by other writers. Despite Gassner's initial acclaim, his practices faced increasing scrutiny and opposition from ecclesiastical authorities, ultimately leading to prohibitions on his exorcisms by Emperor Joseph II and disapproval from Pope Pius VI.

Demonology of the Nineteenth Century

The Enlightenment of the eighteenth century and advancements in scientific understanding alleviated humanity's unfounded fear of the Devil, paving the way for a more objective examination of the subject's historical and philosophical underpinnings in the nineteenth century. Philosophers such as Kant elucidated the principle of evil as a reversal of moral order, while theologians like Daub attempted to construct philosophical interpretations of Satan as the antithesis of goodness.

Schenkel conceptualized Satan as a manifestation within the totality of existence, characterizing him as a collective embodiment of evil. Conversely, Martensen posited Satan as a cosmical principle of temptation, evolving into a concrete personality only through human consciousness. This diversity of perspectives reflected ongoing attempts to reconcile theological doctrines with contemporary philosophical thought.

The dogmatic theology of English and American Protestants maintained traditional beliefs in hell and the Devil, although the practical relevance of these doctrines diminished. Scholars like Schaff and Shedd upheld belief in the Devil's personality based on scriptural evidence, albeit with less emphasis than on other theological doctrines.

In contrast, liberal theology emphasized Jesus' teachings on justice and love, deemphasizing the necessity of belief in the Devil. Critics viewed the concept of a personal Devil as a vestige of pagan polytheism and dualism, attributing its persistence to historical ignorance rather than genuine religious conviction.

Despite lingering beliefs in a personal Devil among orthodox adherents, its influence waned considerably. Theological debates surrounding the Devil's existence reflected shifting philosophical currents, with theologians offering diverse interpretations ranging from allegorical to existential perspectives.

The nineteenth century witnessed a transition from superstition to rational inquiry, with scholars grappling with the complex interplay of theological doctrine, philosophical speculation, and scientific understanding in their attempts to elucidate the nature of evil and its manifestations in human experience.

Present Conditions

In contemporary times, the Roman Catholic Church maintains doctrinal positions similar to those held during the Middle Ages. However, secular authorities now resist any influence from inquisitorial perspectives in legal matters.

Renowned contemporary defenders of the Roman Church, such as Görres, express dissatisfaction with historians who reduce witch prosecutions to mere epidemics. Instead, they attribute the root cause of witchcraft and sorcery to societal apostasy from the Church, which was prevalent during that era. This view, shared by figures like Dr. Haas, acknowledges witchcraft as a revival of pagan beliefs intertwined with distorted Christian notions. Despite recognizing this, proponents like Haas maintain a belief in the actuality of witchcraft, aligning with the perspectives of historical inquisitors and Pope Innocent III.

While the Inquisition, a product of belief in the Devil, is now defunct, remnants of its influence persist. Pope Pius IX and subsequent papal administrations, though lacking operational power, have issued pronouncements against phenomena such as somnambulism and freemasonry, echoing the sentiments of the Inquisition era.

Today, Roman Catholic scholars, reluctant to engage in discussions regarding the Inquisition and the Devil's doctrine, sometimes characterize the Inquisition as a secular institution or defend its actions. However, few are willing to fully condemn the institution or the policies of past popes involved in witch prosecutions.

Though exorcisms and relics such as the holy coat of Treves still hold sway in some Roman Catholic regions, their influence is waning. Moreover, the lingering belief in a personal Devil persists among the uneducated, particularly in Protestant communities.

The Religious Import of Science

The historical episodes of the Inquisition and witch prosecutions underscore the profound influence of religious convictions on ethical conduct. Erroneous religious beliefs, such as dualistic superstitions, can lead to gross moral transgressions. To address this, a comprehensive solution must supplant false religion with truth.

Religion, as the most potent motivator in human affairs, demands rigorous scrutiny. Mysticism and tradition offer inadequate pathways to truth; instead, a commitment to clarity and precision is essential. Pursuing truth through scientific methods, termed the "Religion of Science," yields reliable and verifiable knowledge.

Indeed, science has emerged as a quasi-religious force, gradually displacing dogmatic religious convictions. Scientific truths, universally applicable and demonstrable, have reshaped human civilization, leading to the abolition of practices like witch prosecution. As such, the tenets of science increasingly underpin societal progress and inform global movements toward enlightenment.

In conclusion, the world's conception of reality and progress is increasingly aligned with scientific principles. Any claim to religious validity must ultimately harmonize with scientifically established truths, as science remains the foremost arbiter of universal, orthodox knowledge.

Footnotes:

1. Crosses were ubiquitous, adorning both the attire of individuals and the sky. Additionally, symbols such as crowns of thorns, nails, and scourges were observed. These phenomena prompted the Bishop of Liège to institute special fasts and alert the emperor to the perceived perils facing society.

2. Schlager, in "Wiener Skizzen aus dem Mittelalter," II., n. F., P 35, as referenced by Roskoff, II., p. 294, and König, among others.

3. Hexenprocesse, p. 255.

4. Extracted from the German translation of Weier's "De præstigiis dæmonum," cited in Neue Zusätze.

5. Refer to The New York Evening Post, November 13, 1886, for further information.

6. Occasionally spelled "Thanner," as noted by König, ib., II., p. 572, and Roskoff, II., p. 308.

7. König posits it was a mosquito, while Roskoff suggests a flea.

8. The discovery that Spee von Langenfeld authored the "Cautio criminalis" was made by Leibnitz.

9. Detailed examination is available in Walter Scott's "Letters on Demonology and Witchcraft."

10. Image reproduced from the title page of "Die bezauberte Welt," the first German translation of "De betoverde Weereld."

11. The quotes, along with the subsequent citations, are sourced from J. Scheible's work, Volume I, pages 196 and beyond.

12. Refer to the illustrations on pages 119, 121, and 123 for comparison.

13. Cited from a German translation by Scheible, Volume I, p. 208 and onwards.

14. See the chapter "A Marvellous Experiment with the Imagination of a Hen (Experimentum Mirabile de Imaginatione Gallinæ), in Kircher's "Ars Magna Lucis et Umbræ," Rome, 1646.

15. Refer to Daniel Schwenter's "Deliciæ Physico-Mathematicæ," etc., Nürnberg, 1636.

16. "Die Hexenprocesse, ein culturhistorischer Versuch." Tübingen, 1865.

17. Extracted from Roskoff, p. 239, sourced from "Christliche Mystik," III., 66.

18. "Die Teufelsaustreibung in Werndive. Nach den Berichten des P. Aurelian für das Volk critisch beleuchtet von Richard Treufels." Munich, Schuh & Co., 1892. Note: This work may no longer be readily available in circulation.

19. Refer to Popular Science Monthly, December 1892, p. 161, for additional insights.

17

IN VERSE AND
FABLE

The Devil, as depicted in folklore, commands our admiration for his ceaseless activity. Across various tales, we encounter devil-stones, devil-walls, and other structures attributed to him, suggesting an almost omnipresent and omniscient presence. In popular literature, while he remains the embodiment of physical and moral evil, his role has evolved into that of a general agent of mischief in the universe. He serves as a critic of divine order, fostering discontent and inspiring desires for wealth, power, and knowledge. Often associated with the spirit of progress, he symbolizes both reform and evolution.

Devil-Stories:

The literature on devil-stories is extensive, showcasing a range of narratives. Some legends suggest an origin rooted in hallucination. For instance, tales recount instances where ascetics, isolated from society, experience vivid memories of their past lives, leading to hallucinatory encounters. St. Jerome, in a letter to the virgin Eustochia, candidly describes his own struggles with such hallucinations during his solitary life in the desert.

Another class of stories involves the offspring of the Devil, such as Merlin and Robert the Devil. These tales often revolve around the efforts to either redeem or thwart the diabolical lineage. For instance, Merlin, bestowed with both worldly knowledge and prophetic abilities, uses his gifts to resist his father's influence and align himself with the cause of good. Similarly, Robert the Devil, initially a scourge to society, undergoes a transformative journey of repentance and redemption, ultimately rejecting his infernal heritage.

Not all descendants of the Devil, however, choose the path of righteousness. Characters like Eggelino and Alberico succumb to their malevolent lineage, wreaking havoc and meeting tragic ends. The stories of such figures serve as cautionary tales about the consequences of yielding to evil impulses.

The legend of St. Dagobert's salvation, depicted in a bas-relief at the church of St. Denys, illustrates the redemptive power of Christian faith. According to the legend, the prayers of a hermit, guided by divine intervention, rescue the soul of King Dagobert from the clutches of demons, underscoring the triumph of faith over evil forces.

Numerous romances, such as Spenser's Faerie Queene and Bunyan's Pilgrim's Progress, depict the perennial struggle between man and the forces of darkness. These allegorical tales, while originating in the sixteenth and seventeenth centuries, trace their thematic roots to earlier works like Le Romant des trois Pélerinages, which chronicles a pilgrim's journey through life and encounters with various manifestations of temptation and corruption.

In sum, devil-stories encompass a rich tapestry of narratives, exploring themes of temptation, redemption, and the eternal struggle between good and evil. They offer insights into human nature and the enduring quest for spiritual enlightenment amidst the shadows of darkness.

Devil-Contracts:

The Devil, in his struggle against God for the souls of mankind, was believed to possess a particular affinity for acquiring souls. As the ruler of the world, he could readily fulfill even the most extravagant desires and was sometimes willing to pay a steep price when individuals pledged themselves to him for eternity. Thus, the concept of making compacts with the Devil emerged, with the Devil taking great care to establish his claim to the human soul through meticulously crafted legal documents. Despite his reputation as a deceiver, there is no known instance in devil lore where the Devil attempts to deceive those with whom he makes pacts. This paradox paints him as a figure unfairly maligned and even as a martyr of straightforward honesty.

The oldest tale of a devil-contract is the legend of Theophilus, recounted by Eutychian. Theophilus, a pious man initially elected as bishop but later deprived of his position unjustly, enters into a pact with Satan out of desperation. However, he ultimately repents, seeks absolution, and is granted forgiveness by the Holy Virgin. Even popes, such as Pope Sylvester II, were rumored to have made pacts with the Devil, although the historical veracity of such stories remains debated.

The most renowned story among devil-contracts is the saga of Dr. Johannes Faustus. Whether Faust was a historical figure or merely a literary invention is uncertain, but his tale became a focal point for various traditions surrounding wizards and intellectuals. The Faust legend, originating from a Roman Catholic perspective, portrays Faust as an individual who allies himself with the Devil, practices magic, and ultimately pays for his actions with his soul. Faust embodies the spirit of natural science, historical inquiry, and modern discoveries, leading to his subjugation of nature and revival of ancient heroes and ideals.

In the context of medieval times, progress and the pursuit of knowledge were often equated with sorcery and condemned as the work of Satan. The example of Roger Bacon illustrates this point, as his scientific experiments were met with fear and suspicion, highlighting the prevailing belief that delving into the mysteries of nature bordered on witchcraft.

The Faust Legend:

Faust epitomizes the pursuit of scientific inquiry amidst spiritual peril. He delves into the mysteries of nature, risking condemnation for eternity, yet remains undeterred in his quest for knowledge. Medieval theology attributed Satan's fall to ambitious pride, yet Faust boldly defies this cautionary tale by seeking enlightenment forbidden by divine decree. In Marlowe's "Faustus," Lucifer's hubris precedes his downfall, a theme echoed in Faust's dialogue with Mephistopheles, where Faust extols his own fortitude and dismisses the allure of heavenly joys.

The earliest known account of Faust, dating back to 1587 and known as the Volksbuch, survives in a single copy now housed in Ulm. According to its preface, the manuscript was obtained from a friend in Speyer, originally written in Latin. Faust, depicted as a farmer's son near Weimar, embarks on theological studies at Wittenberg. Driven by an insatiable desire for omniscience and omnipotence akin to God, he turns to the occult. Despite mastering demonic forces, Faust remains defiant, even rebuffing the Devil's warnings of damnation.

Faust's pact with Mephistopheles, sealed with Faust's own blood, sets the stage for his tumultuous journey. Mephistopheles indulges Faust with illusions, lavish gifts, and carnal pleasures, leading Faust into moral decay. Their discussions touch on eschatological themes, revealing Faust's ambition to unravel nature's secrets and transcend earthly bounds. Faust's travels span from infernal realms to heavenly heights, offering glimpses into the afterlife and celestial wonders.

As Faust's fateful deadline approaches, melancholy descends upon him. On the eve of his pact's expiration, a gruesome fate befalls him, witnessed only by fearful onlookers. Faust's tragic demise marks the end of his mortal coil, leaving behind a legacy of arcane knowledge and moral ambiguity.

Subsequent iterations of the Faust legend, including adaptations by Widman and Pfitzer, contributed to its enduring cultural significance. From puppet shows to Marlowe's theatrical interpretation, Faust captivated audiences across Europe, inspiring literary masterpieces like Goethe's seminal work, solidifying Faust's status as an enduring icon of human ambition and existential inquiry.

Goethe's Faust:

Goethe's portrayal of Faust aligns with Protestant ideology. Faust aligns himself with the spirit of negation, bargaining his soul's fate in pursuit of fulfillment. However, he finds no solace in the offerings of this negating force. Instead, Faust discovers contentment through purposeful endeavors for the betterment of humanity, transcending the influence of negativity embodied by Mephistopheles. While Faust inherits the revolutionary fervor of his time, embracing a love for liberty, he ultimately finds salvation through his altruistic actions.

The character of Mephistopheles evolves beyond a mere embodiment of malevolence in Goethe's rendition. His negation transforms into a critical spirit, prompting constructive endeavors. Thus, Faust emerges as a symbol of bold inquiry and progressive ideals characteristic of the modern era.

In contrast to the Volksbuch's literal depiction of the Devil as a feared entity, Goethe employs allegory to imbue the story with symbolic meaning. This shift is evident in scenes like the Walpurgis night, which satirically reflects contemporary societal norms.

The diminishing awe surrounding the figure of the Devil is evident in literary works following the Middle Ages. Hans Sachs portrays the Devil as a figure of mockery, challenging the notion of his power. Dionysius Klein adopts a humorous perspective on the Devil, marking a departure from earlier solemn portrayals. As societal beliefs evolve, the Devil transitions from a feared entity to a symbol of evil principles.

Modern interpretations of the Devil in literature, such as Victor Hugo's political satire, depict him as a figure of ridicule rather than fear. This trend is further exemplified in works like Lesage's "The Devil on Two Sticks," where the Devil becomes a subject of amusement. Heinrich Heine's lighthearted portrayal of Satan reflects a similar departure from earlier solemnity, presenting him as a charming and witty character.

Contemporary literature, as seen in works like "Hell Up to Date," continues to explore the Devil's character in a satirical manner. Through humorous depictions, the Devil becomes a source of entertainment rather than dread. These stories reflect a departure from literal interpretations of Christian mythology, transforming into symbolic narratives that reflect societal attitudes and values.

Footnotes:

1. References to historical sources such as "Gesta Dagob." (cc. 23, 44), Baronius (647, 5), D. Bouquet's "Rec. des histoires

de France," and Didron's "Christian Iconography" provide additional context and verification for the discussed topics.

2. An old English translation of the text mentioned is preserved in the University Library of Cambridge, England.

3. The illustrations accompanying the text, including the depiction of the storm during Faust's funeral, Wagner inheriting Faust's possessions, and Faust's ghost haunting Wittenberg, offer visual representations of the narrative.

4. The translation of Victor Hugo's verses provided in this text is a specially made rendition by E. F. L Gauss.

18

THE PHILOSOPHICAL PROBLEM OF GOOD AND EVIL

The inquiry into the essence of evil stands as paramount among philosophical, religious, and moral deliberations. The inherent presence of suffering pervades existence, shaping its character while simultaneously giving rise to fundamental blessings that confer meaning upon life. Pain serves as the impetus for introspection and inquiry; a state of unbroken contentment would render reflection and innovation superfluous. Mortality engenders the yearning for an existence beyond the grave; without death, the concept of religion would hold no sway. Similarly, sin imbues virtue with value;

without the possibility of transgression, the pursuit of righteousness would lack significance. In the absence of adversity and imperfection, ideals, progress, and the aspiration towards loftier objectives would find no footing.

The Mythology of Evil

Given mythology's perennial appeal as a form of metaphysical discourse, it is unsurprising that the notion of evil has been personified across cultures. Virtually every religious tradition features malevolent entities or dark forces symbolizing pain, despair, and ruin. In ancient Egypt, fearsome deities such as Set or Seth, Bess, and Typhon epitomized the forces of darkness. While the gods of ancient Brahmanism were not starkly delineated into good and evil, the triumph of Mahâmâya, the great goddess, over Mahisha, the giant king, underscored the victory of light over darkness. Buddhists attribute the personification of evil to Mâra, the tempter and harbinger of sin and death. Chaldean lore personifies chaos in Tiamat, the primordial monster of the abyss. In Persian mythology, Angra Mainyu or Ahriman embodies the forces of darkness and mischief. Jewish tradition identifies Satan as the adversary, while early Christians referred to him as the Devil, signifying slanderer due to his false accusations against humanity, as depicted in the story of Job. Norse mythology portrays Loki as the trickster figure embodying malevolence. Throughout history, various cultures have developed extensive demonologies, with Japanese and Chinese traditions boasting particularly elaborate depictions of malevolent beings.

The evolution of the concept of evil as a personification constitutes a captivating chapter in human history, characterized by nuanced shifts and reinterpretations over time. While vestiges of ancient pagan beliefs endure in Hebrew and Christian demonologies, subsequent eras have witnessed the incorporation of new elements and interpretations. Franz Xaver Kraus notes the divergence between early Christian depictions of demons and contemporary conceptions, highlighting the evolution of symbolic representations such as the serpent or dragon as embodiments of evil. The intellectual development of humanity proceeds through incremental progress, with old ideas undergoing transformation rather than wholesale abandonment. Notably, Gunkel's scholarship illustrates how biblical descriptions of Leviathan and God's confrontation with sea monsters draw upon Chaldean mythology, underscoring the persistence of historical continuity amid evolving religious beliefs.

The depiction of evil and its personifications, while at times laced with elements of humor, often carries weighty implications, particularly evident in narratives surrounding witch persecution. Nonetheless, the enduring allure of the Devil underscores his enduring cultural significance, predating even the most ancient European aristocracies and royal lineages, and surpassing the antiquity of biblical narratives and architectural marvels such as the Pyramids.

With the historical context of the Devil delineated in previous chapters, our discourse now turns to a philosophical exploration of the concept of evil, wherein the objective existence of evil stands as the foremost consideration.

The Age of Subjectivism

The inquiry arises: "Is evil merely an illusion, a relative concept to be discarded as a biased view of reality? Does it persist solely due to our subjective perspectives, destined to vanish upon our apprehension of the world in its objective truth?" The prevailing trend to perceive evil as a purely negative notion resonates with the contemporary ethos and stands as one of the prevailing convictions of our time.

In antiquity, humanity habitually externalized the various impulses and aspirations of the soul. The Greek pursuit of beauty found embodiment in the ideal of Aphrodite, while the moral imperative of righteousness manifested to the Jew as Yahveh, the Lawgiver of Mount Sinai. Religious fervor found expression through ceremonial rites and ecclesiastical institutions.

This paradigm shifted with the advent of what is commonly termed modern history, marked by innovations such as gunpowder, the compass, and printing, culminating in the discovery of America and the Reformation at the close of the fifteenth century. As humanity's horizon expanded, so too did the recognition of individual subjectivity. Philosophical and religious thought, from Descartes to Luther, increasingly centered on the individual consciousness. Religion came to be seen as an internal, rather than external, force, with conscience assuming primacy in matters of conduct. Tolerance became imperative, and subjectivity became the cornerstone of public and private life. Thus, the Reformation era emerged as a revolutionary movement challenging the traditional authority of external objectivity, asserting the primacy of individualism and subjectivity.

While the architects of this movement did not intend to wholly discard objective authority, the spirit of nominalism that pervaded them ultimately dominated their trajectory. Descartes, with his assertion "Cogito, ergo sum," unwittingly laid the groundwork for a radical interpretation of subjectivity, albeit assuming objective existence on a trivial premise. Similarly, Luther, with his rigid upbringing and steadfast narrowness, while not inherently predisposed to later theories rooted in subjective conscience, nonetheless paved the way for the consequences of acknowledging the supremacy of subjective principle. This trajectory ultimately culminated in a denial of objective authority across philosophical, political, religious, and ethical domains, manifesting as anarchism in politics, agnosticism in philosophy, and ethical relativism or intuitionism in ethics.

Our contemporary civilization is founded upon the Protestant ideal of individualism, reaping considerable benefits. However, we must guard against the inherent one-sidedness of subjectivism. Objectivism, though seemingly flawed from the vantage point of modern subjectivism, is not inherently erroneous. The external methodologies of the Roman Church and the tyranny of its hierarchical system, which substituted priestly authority and an infallible papacy for divine authority, are misguided. Protestantism's primary task lay in challenging this authority, rooted in the fallible human authority of mortals. However, many Protestant affirmations merely echo the old Romanism, constraining conscience and stifling reasoning. True progress lay in the advent of Science, the positive force destined to build a new civilization.

Protestantism, therefore, does not represent the final word in the religious evolution of humanity. Higher aims and more positive outcomes necessitate a reevaluation of the importance of objectivity. Humanity need not revert to the dogmatic systems of hierarchical institutions but must recognize that truth is not solely a subjective conception. Truth embodies an objective element, established through methodical critique and grounded in evidence. Objective truth, as discerned through science, represents the highest revelation of God, surpassing dogmatic teachings and individual perceptions. Faith in the objective authority of truth heralds the next step in religious evolution, ushering in an era of scientific objectivism marked by constructive pragmatism.

Is Evil a Positive Phenomenon?

In a modern allegory, the relativity of good and evil is depicted through the tale of a farmer who, while tending his field with a cultivator, curses the morning-glories encroaching upon his maize stalks as creations of the Devil. Meanwhile, his daughter, weaving a wreath of the same flowers, admires the beauty of God's creation. While good and evil may indeed be relative, this relativity does not imply nonexistence. Relationships, including those between good and evil, are factual occurrences. If mischief arises from the misplacement of good things, the resultant evil does not become illusory but retains its positiveness as any other reality.

Similarly, the relativity of knowledge does not signify,

as some agnostic philosophers suggest, the impossibility of knowledge. Material bodies like stones are not the sole realities; relationships also hold tangible existence, and under varying circumstances, the same entity may exhibit qualities of both good and evil.

Rather than undermining the objectivity of the moral ideal, a proper understanding of the relativity of goodness and badness serves as a potent catalyst for realizing goodness. Indeed, there should be nothing so detrimental that, with prudent management, it cannot be harnessed for positive ends. Despite this, badness is sometimes characterized as a mere negation, with assertions made regarding its lack of positive impact. Bertha von Suttner, an advocate for universal peace, echoes this sentiment in her work "The Inventory of a Soul," where she discusses "The Principle of Evil as a Phantom." Von Suttner contends:

"I do not believe in the phantoms of badness, misery, and death. They are mere shadows, zeros, nothingnesses. They are negations of real things, but not real things themselves... There is light, but there is no darkness: darkness is only the non-existence of light. There is life, death is only a local ceasing of life-phenomena... We grant that Ormuzd and Ahriman, God and Devil, are at least thinkable, but there are other opposites in which it is apparent that one is the non-existence of the other. For instance: noise and silence. Think of a silence so powerful as to suppress a noise... Darkness has no degree, while light has. There is more light or less light, but various shades of darkness can mean only little or less light. Thus, life is a magnitude, but death is a zero. Something and nothing cannot be in struggle with each other.

Nothing is without arms, nothing as an independent idea is only an abortion of human weaknesses... two are necessary to produce struggle. If I am in the room, I am here; if I leave it, I am no longer here. There can be no quarrel between my ego-present and ego-absent."

This assertion, while forceful, represents a sophisticated denial of evil's existence, rooted in the negativism prevalent in philosophy from Descartes to Spencer. Despite its consistency as monism, it cannot be unequivocally accepted.

Indeed, while the concept of a personal Devil is as fantastical as a fairy or an elf, and there exists no intrinsic evil or goodness, the dualism posited by the Manichees is unsustainable. The principle of evil cannot be conceived as an independent substance or entity. However, this does not negate its real and positive existence. While silence may represent the absence of noise, noise is not inherently good, nor is silence inherently bad. Depending on context, silence may be detrimental, and a lie is more than just the absence of truth. The absence of food may be a negation, but viewed in relation to hunger, it becomes a tangible experience. Sickness, too, may seem like the absence of health, yet it arises from tangible causes or influences. Similarly, a debt may represent a negative on one's ledger but constitutes a positive for the creditor.

If negative concepts were mere manifestations of human frailty, as von Suttner argues, mathematicians would have no use for the minus sign. Likewise, if the idea of evil were baseless superstition, its enduring influence on humanity would be inexplicable. While all existence may be inherently positive, it is essential to recognize that existence, in the abstract, is neither inherently good nor bad; rather, goodness and badness are contingent upon the relationships between existent entities. Some entities may negate others, leading to conflicts. Parasites, for instance, sustain themselves at the expense of other lives, and such negations represent tangible realities that neutralize the actions of other entities.

The concept of goodness does not equate to mere existence, nor does badness denote non-existence. Existence represents the ultimate reality, comprising the entirety of being. However, good and evil, viewed from a specific perspective, constitute contrasting features, both of which are actualities. The question remains whether our individual standpoint represents the positive one, with all opposing forces deemed negative or evil.

It stands to reason that every being would naturally regard its own standpoint as positive, with any force that undermines it labeled as negative. Nevertheless, while subjectivism may form the initial stage of ethical valuation, it cannot serve as the ultimate solution to the problem of good and evil.

Is There an Objective Standard of Goodness?

If we were to define good simply as that which brings pleasure or enhances one's life, and bad as that which causes pain or threatens destruction, then the standard of goodness and badness would be entirely subjective. An anecdote featuring a savage chief, as recounted by Tylor and subsequently Spencer, illustrates this concept, where the chief deemed an action bad if it affected him negatively but good if it benefited him. In such a scenario, goodness would be relative to individual perspectives, lacking any objective value.

This viewpoint, which grounds ethics in the pursuit of pleasure and avoidance of pain, is known as hedonism. In its crudest form, as articulated by Bentham, hedonism prioritizes individual pleasure and interprets altruism as refined egotism. According to this perspective, altruism is seen as merely loving oneself in others.

It's important to note that even the intuitionist, who grounds ethics in the dictates of conscience, ultimately falls into a form of subjectivism. The intuitionist finds moral authority within themselves, in the form of their conscience, which dictates what they perceive as ethical. While differing from Bentham's hedonism in emphasizing the pleasure of conscience over sensory pleasures, intuitionism remains fundamentally subjective.

Even modern utilitarianism, as exemplified by Spencer, fails to establish an objective ethical framework. By advocating for the greatest happiness of the greatest number as the ethical maxim, modern utilitarianism merely aggregates individual subjectivities without introducing an objective principle. Consequently, subjective ethical principles persist, akin to the worldview of Tylor's savage.

However, subjective ethical theories overlook a crucial aspect of ethics: its objectivity. Indeed, ethics inherently possesses an objective nature. If moral conduct lacks an objective authority, then ethics would amount to little more than an illusion, reducing morality to a mere calculation of pleasures and pains—a soulless dietetics.

Yet, empirical evidence demonstrates an objective

authority for conduct in life. Just as the laws of nature govern the physical realm, ethical principles guide human behavior within the cosmic order. This cosmic order, akin to the concept of evolution postulated by Darwin, delineates a definitive path for individual and collective progress. Those who align with this path progress harmoniously, while those who resist face natural consequences.

In this cosmic scheme, morality transcends the mere pursuit of pleasure or avoidance of pain. Rather, morality aligns with the laws of evolution, guiding individuals towards voluntary actions necessary for progress, irrespective of personal preferences.

Ethics, therefore, hinges on duty, characterized by its objective reality, unwavering sternness, and authoritative nature. A good action isn't moral because it brings pleasure but because it conforms to duty. Thus, the pursuit of pleasure shouldn't be the aim; instead, true fulfillment lies in aligning with the demands of the cosmic order, or what some might call God's will.

Critically, those denying an objective norm of right and wrong tend to overlook humanity's survival, not because of immorality, but precisely due to adherence to ethical principles. This is evident in comparing human behavior to that of animals, like wolves, who survive without moral considerations. Yet, humans, despite slaughtering animals for sustenance, endure and thrive due to the ethical considerations inherent in their actions.

Indeed, the slaughter of animals, while morally complex, serves a purpose beyond mere sustenance—it reflects a willingness to sacrifice lower life for higher life. Thus, the evaluation of actions must extend beyond subjective morality to consider their alignment with the cosmic order and their contribution to progress.

Ultimately, ethics isn't defined by the pursuit of pleasure or avoidance of pain; rather, it's characterized by adherence to duty and alignment with the laws of evolution. This objective standard of goodness transcends individual preferences and guides individuals towards true fulfillment and progress.

Religion has historically played a significant role in shaping ethical frameworks and understanding the nature of the cosmos. However, the interpretation of religious concepts has varied widely across cultures and individuals, leading to diverse conceptions of God and morality.

God, often depicted as the ultimate authority for conduct, represents more than just goodness. While some may anthropomorphize God as inherently good, it's essential to recognize that God transcends moral categories. Rather, God serves as the standard of goodness, with creatures being deemed good to the extent that they reflect God's will and adhere to moral principles.

The relationship between God and the universe is complex. While God is not synonymous with existence itself, God's influence permeates every aspect of reality, conditioning the cosmic order and serving as the ultimate criterion for morality. In this sense, God represents the supernatural aspect of existence, providing a framework for understanding and adhering to moral principles.

Throughout history, different cultures have depicted God in various forms, reflecting their unique interpretations and understandings. From the bloodthirsty chieftain of primitive societies to the benevolent father figure of modern religions, the concept of God evolves alongside human consciousness and societal development.

Similarly, the depiction of Satan, as the embodiment of rebellion and tyranny, contrasts with the concept of God as the source of liberty and order. While Satan represents the misguided pursuit of independence through rebellion, God symbolizes true freedom attained through self-control, adherence to moral principles, and alignment with the cosmic order.

In essence, religion serves as a vehicle for exploring and understanding moral truths, albeit through the lens of mythological imagery and allegory. As science advances and humanity's understanding of the cosmos deepens, religious concepts evolve, gradually transitioning from myth to knowledge. This evolution reflects humanity's ongoing quest for truth, freedom, and moral enlightenment.

Ultimately, true religion embodies a love of truth and a pursuit of independence, empowering individuals to align with moral principles and contribute to the progress of humanity. By embracing the truth and striving for moral excellence, individuals can transcend subjective notions of morality and align with the objective standard of goodness inherent in the cosmic order.

The Concept of God

God, a term deeply rooted in religious discourse, is often asserted to lie beyond the purview of scientific inquiry. Both religious agnostics and infidel agnostics, influenced by nominalistic subjectivism, find themselves in a dichotomy where their beliefs or disbeliefs lack rationality. If an objective authority for moral conduct exists, it should be comprehensible; obedience can only follow understanding. Empirical observation indicates the presence of such an authority, with evolutionary theory poised to substantiate this claim through empirical evidence. Termed "God" in religious discourse, scientists encapsulate this authoritative aspect within the framework of "laws of nature." Each natural law, serving as a stringent guide for conduct within its domain, is inherently linked to the essence of God.

Of paramount importance within the ethical realm are the laws regulating human interactions, intricately weaving destinies and fostering mutual support. Existence, viewed as a harmonious whole, encompasses every entity as an integral part, with the collective unity constituting the essence of each creature's being. This interconnectedness manifests as a universal longing for completeness, echoing across diverse religious traditions. Emerson's words underscore this sentiment, emphasizing the intrinsic interdependence among all entities.

The unity and coherence permeating existence transcend mere theoretical constructs, representing an observable reality. Science elucidates the cosmos as a comprehensible order governed by immutable laws, challenging notions of chaos and incomprehensibility. This ordered cosmos facilitates the emergence of intelligence, paving the way for sentient beings to evolve into rational minds. God, as the foundational principle engendering reason, transforms individuals into persons, imbuing them with the capacity for rational thought and moral agency.

Thus, beings are deemed "good" to the extent that they mirror the image of God. Contrary to misconceptions, the essence of progress lies not in increasing heterogeneity but in nurturing the growth of the soul. Evolution transcends mere adaptation, culminating in the progressive embodiment of truth. Ethical progress, consequently, stems from adherence to right conduct rather than mere environmental adaptation.

Every facet of human experience serves as a revelation, with moral truths holding particular significance. Despite primitive interpretations, these truths exert a formative influence on the soul's development. As humanity's understanding evolves, mythological allegories gradually yield to rational comprehension, symbolizing a transition from superstition to knowledge.

God, often attributed with qualities of goodness, surpasses mere moral categorization. While anthropomorphizing God as inherently good is common, God transcends such labels, serving as the ultimate standard for morality. Creatures attain goodness by aligning with God's will, discerned through empirical revelations or what science terms "experiences" formulated as laws of nature.

God, distinct from existence itself, represents the normative essence shaping the cosmic order. This distinction between God and the totality of existence upholds monotheism while acknowledging the intrinsic connection between God and the cosmos. As the foundational principle conditioning reality, God's omnipresence underscores the inherent authority guiding moral conduct.

Supernaturalism, though redefined, retains its validity, recognizing God as the fundamental rationale behind existence's orderliness. Despite differing conceptions, the recognition of a higher authority underpinning reality remains immutable, transcending cultural and philosophical variations.

In contrast to Satan's rebellious nature, symbolizing false freedom and tyranny, God epitomizes genuine liberty grounded in self-control and adherence to universal principles. Satan's promise of independence through defiance contrasts sharply with God's bestowal of freedom through moral rectitude. Embracing truth as the pathway to freedom, individuals transcend the illusion of dependence, attaining true independence through alignment with moral and philosophical truths.

In essence, true religion champions the pursuit of truth and freedom, aligning with moral principles and fostering individual development. While interpretations of God vary, reflecting diverse mental and moral dispositions, the essence of divinity transcends subjective perceptions, embodying the ultimate standard of morality and freedom.

The Devil Concept in Relation to the Concept of God

The development of the concept of evil holds significant relevance in the historical narrative of religion, as an individual's perception of Satan often reflects their mental and moral disposition.

While biblical teachings assert humanity's creation in the image of God, anthropological insights suggest that individuals construct their gods in their own likeness. Indeed, every conception of God bears the imprint of its adherent's character. It has been aptly remarked that understanding one's conception of God provides insight into their own identity.

Similarly, the conception of the Devil mirrors this principle, offering a window into one's psyche. In essence, the perception of Satan is intimately intertwined with the individual's worldview and moral framework.

There exists a striking resemblance between conceptions of good and evil, suggesting a natural inclination towards a certain thematic consistency in human thought. Notably, one's understanding of the Devil often mirrors their conception of God. Comparing iconic representations of God holding the universe with depictions of Mara, the Buddhist Satan, grasping the world-wheel illustrates this parallelism.

Historically, evidence supports the existence of Trinity conceptions for both God and Satan. Just as pagan deities were characterized by trinities, such as the three-headed Hecuba, Christian art similarly portrays trinitarian representations of both divine and demonic figures. This motif possibly originated from the adaptation of the two-headed Janus.

The Christian notion of Satan as a three-headed monster finds resonance in ancient texts and artwork, symbolizing malevolence and chaos. Dante's vivid description of the three-faced Satan further exemplifies this concept, portraying him as a grotesque figure embodying torment and despair.

In Christian theology, Satan assumes various forms, including that of a dragon or an ominous figure resembling an African or Ethiopian. Such representations, found in the writings of Augustine and Gregory the Great, reflect medieval perceptions of evil as grotesque and deformed.

Comparing literary depictions of Satan, such as Milton's heroic figure and Goethe's philosophical Mephistopheles, reveals cultural nuances and philosophical underpinnings. While Milton's Satan embodies rebellion and dissent, Goethe's Mephistopheles represents the spirit of criticism and skepticism, engaging in intellectual discourse with the divine.

The relationship between God and the Devil is complex, occasionally necessitating mutual acknowledgment and interaction. As portrayed in Goethe's "Faust," even Satan acknowledges the occasional need for rapport with the divine, underscoring the nuanced dynamic between good and evil in human existence.

Conclusion

Initially, the concept of evil personified may evoke repulsion, yet upon closer examination, the persona of the Devil becomes increasingly intriguing. Initially characterized as the embodiment of unpleasantness, the Evil One evolves into the symbol of all that is malevolent, immoral, and destructive. He represents hatred, annihilation, and opposition to the divine order.

The Devil emerges as the rebel against cosmic order, challenging the uniformity and harmony of the universe. His existence introduces dissonance and unpredictability, disrupting the prescribed course of events. Paradoxically, this opposition serves as a catalyst for progress and individuality, preventing the stagnation that would ensue from absolute conformity.

The question of why God does not eliminate the Devil may seem whimsical, yet it underscores a fundamental truth: the existence of evil is intrinsic to the divine order. Without the concept of evil, the notion of goodness loses its significance, and the dynamic interplay between God and the Devil ceases.

The universe, by its very nature, requires resistance for growth and evolution to occur. Struggles against adversity stimulate progress and inspire moral aspirations. Pain and deficiencies fuel the desire for improvement, instigating the pursuit of higher ideals and the advancement of civilization.

The figure of Satan, often vilified, possesses redeeming qualities that merit acknowledgment. Despite his association with wrongdoing, Satan embodies rebellion, progress, and the pursuit of knowledge. He challenges societal norms and inspires innovation, often at great personal cost.

Moreover, Satan's unwavering integrity, as depicted in folklore and literature, serves as a testament to his character. Even his adversaries acknowledge his steadfastness, highlighting his reliability and honor in fulfilling his promises.

In examining our own nature, we may find parallels between ourselves and the Devil. While not condoning egregious transgressions, we recognize our inclination towards mischief and rebellion. These traits, though often frowned upon, contribute to the richness and complexity of human experience.

Ultimately, the existence of evil, temptation, and sin serves a purpose in the divine plan. They challenge and instruct humanity, prompting reflection and moral growth. Even in the presence of evil, the divine essence permeates all aspects of existence, imparting wisdom and guiding human endeavor.

In this light, the Devil emerges as an indispensable component of the divine order, facilitating growth, resilience, and spiritual enlightenment. Indeed, even in the realm of darkness, the presence of God is palpable, imbuing every aspect of existence with purpose and meaning.

Footnotes

1. An Egyptian Devil, depicted in Montfaucon's works, features a human head with six animal heads protruding from it: one of an ox, one of a bird, and four others resembling serpents.

2. Regarding the myth of Mahâmâya's origin, identified with Durgâ, it is detailed in "the Chandi" within the Mârkandeya Purâna. Vishnu, witnessing the plight of the gods due to the giant-king Mahisha, emanated streams of glory from his countenance, forming Mahâmâya. Similar effulgences emerged from other gods, merging into the goddess, who then vanquished the buffalo-shaped monster Mahisha. Another version of this myth is found in the Vâmana Purâna. For further information, refer to Hindu mythologies under Mahisha and Mahishamardini.

3. Didron, Chr. Icon., II., p. 119 (Refer to pages 468 and 469 of this work).

4. A Persian Devil depicted in the Didron collection appears as a man adorned with necklaces, bracelets, and anklets, yet with claws on his heels and toes, and horns on his head. Named Ahriman, Spirit of Darkness, he is the

Iranian adversary of Ormuzd, the second-born of the Eternal One, akin to Ormuzd as an emanation from the Primal Light. Equally pure but ambitious and proud, he became envious of God's first-born. -- Didron, Iconography, II., p. 122.

5. From a Turkish manuscript obtained by Napoleon I. in Cairo and gifted to the National Library in Paris (S.C. 242). Its author, Saïaidi Mahammed ebu emer Hassan esseoudi (990an), describes the depicted monster as having olive-colored flesh, green eyes with red pupils, and a red tongue. He wears a green scarf, pale purple trousers lined with blue, and gold necklaces and armlets. -- Didron, Iconography, II., 122.

6. From Kugler's Italian Schools of Painting.

7. Geschichte der christlichen Kunst, Vol. I., p. 210.

8. "A dragon of marvellous size lying under the very steps."

9. Schöpfung und Chaos. Göttingen, 1891.

10. The notable aspect of this painting lies not only in the inclusion of the Virgin Mary on the throne of the Trinity, a common motif, but in the dual presence of Christ as both a grown man and an infant.

11. Inventarium einer Seele. Chap. XV.

12. This exposition was initially published in The Monist, Vol. VI, No. 4, pp. 585 ff. In response, Baroness Bertha von Suttner expressed courteous acknowledgment, suggesting potential acceptance of the author's arguments.

13. Tylor, Primitive Culture, Vol. II., p. 318.

14. Cf. Homilies of Science, "The Test of Progress," p. 36, and "The Ethics of Evolution," p. 41.

15. Pantheism equates God with the All. Nomotheism posits that the laws of nature are not external decrees but manifestations of God. Monotheism asserts the existence of

one personal God. See the author's Religion of Science, pp. 19 et seq., The Authority for Conduct.

16. See the illustration on page 441.

17. Didron, Icon. Chr., pages 25 and 64.

18. This conception of Serapis resembles Cerberus, as noted by Manobius (Sal., I. 20), who states that Cerberus has the heads of a lion, a wolf, and a dog. See Menzel, Vorchr. Unsterblichkeitslehre, II., p. 5.

19. This fresco embodies the Christian worldview of the fourteenth century. A sonnet accompanying the fresco explains that nine choirs of angels surround the world, with constellations revolving around the earth at its center.

20. This picture is part of the depiction of Hades presented on page 194.

21. Compare page 164.

22. The inscription reads "Seel Lucifer mâtre (i.e., maistre) d'abisme d'enfer."